CW00646379

A book that cuts to the truth of the acting industry- written from an outsider's point of view. Catherine Balavage grew up in a small Scottish town without either the proper training, or industry contacts prior to her career.

The book includes advice from casting directors Amy Hubbard and Richard Evans, actor Andrew Tiernan and an exclusive interview with Spotlight amongst interviews with countless other industry professionals.

It is an essential for anyone who wants to be an actor.

"Essential reading for anyone about to springboard into an exciting project; clear, friendly and accessible" Margaret Graham, author.

"Catherine's determination to succeed in a fiercely-competitive industry is unrivalled - I'm genuinely delighted that she has decided to share this essential knowledge and experience with How To Be a Successful Actor: Becoming an Actorpreneur." Jack Bowman, actor and associate director of the Lost Theatre.

"A must-have resource for anyone thinking of becoming an actor." Penny Deacon, author.

"First published in 2014

ISBN 978-0-9929639-2-7

How To Be A Successful Actor. Becoming an Actorpreneur.

CONTENTS

How To Be A Successful Actor. Becoming an Actorpreneur.

Introduction.

I had the idea for this book years ago. I had read a lot of acting books and although they were not all bad, I found it hard to relate to them. A lot of them were written by much older men and one even discussed whether women should wear trouser in an audition! They didn't seem to capture the world of acting or even tell you how to actually become an actor. I was constantly asked about how someone becomes an actor and that is when the idea crystallised: I could write down all of the stuff it took me years to learn, effectively saving aspiring actors hours of research and years of mistakes. It would be written by an actual actor, who has been in the trenches of acting for over a decade. In short: it would be the book I wish I could have read when I started acting.

In the spirit of a true procrastinator, it took me four years to start writing it. In those years I lost count of how many times I have been asked for acting advice. Sometimes more than five times a day and by a wide variety of people, from surgeons to police officers, everyone, it seems, has some desire to be an actor.

At first I was bemused by this. I am a working actor but not a household name. But I know what I am doing. I worked my way up from nothing. I knew no-one in the industry when I started. I didn't go to RADA, I didn't even know anyone in London before I moved there. Nor did I have a job or somewhere to live. In fact, I came from a small Scottish town. I did not know what Spotlight was or how I would ever work up the courage to audition. But I did. I found the courage, the knowledge and met the right people. Ten years later. I have built my acting career up from nothing.

It surprises me when I meet some people on film sets or in the theatre and they have not researched the industry they want to be in at all. When I decided to start taking acting seriously I spent hours on the internet looking for advice and sending letters off to casting directors and agents. It took a long time, and many years of mistakes and hard work, to get where I am today: a working actor. You can skip all of that hard work, the trial and error; you just need to read this book.

This book is for people who are serious about their career; it is for the beginner and also for those who have already started acting. There is some good advice from the top people in the industry as well as interviews with them. I will go over the basics but I will not bore you with them. I hope you find this book as entertaining as you do educational, and I wish you all the best with your acting career.

How To Be A Successful Actor. Becoming an Actorpreneur.

Chapter 1: In The Beginning

The first thing you should do is find out if acting is actually for you. A lot of people like the idea of acting but the reality is very different. Not only is there massive unemployment but it is just not as glamorous as people think it is. You spend most of your time on set waiting for your turn to film your scene. It can be boring and tedious, and that is when you actually have a job. It is very hurry up and wait.

Then there is the matter of talent. When I started acting I thought everyone could do it, but now I know that this is just not true.

Make sure you really want to act, join an extras agency and spend a day on set, or try and get a part in some amateur or community theatre.

The most common advice I received when I asked actors what career advice they would give to people who wanted to break into the acting business was: *don't*. This is not (just) because they want less competition, but also the knowledge that it is an unforgiving profession that takes more than it gives. Sorry to be pessimistic, but it is important to know what you are letting yourself in for. An acting career can be amazing and fulfilling. You can become a millionaire and travel all around the world, but it is important to know that an estimated ninety-eight percent of actors are out of work at any one time. Pay is also atrocious. It may be okay to be young and poor but as you get older the poverty will start to bite. Especially as your friends and family will be doing well in their careers and getting on with their lives. To be successful in acting you have to give yourself over to it like a nun.

If you are a woman the odds are even less forgiving. There are three roles for every male compared with one for every women. The odds get even worse as a woman gets older. Acting also has a high dropout rate. As people's twenties run out it can be difficult to keep the momentum up and stay positive. In our youth-obsessed culture it can destroy people if they are not successful by the age of thirty. It is important to remember that a lot of people who became successful did not get their first roles when they were teenagers. Annette Benning was 30 years old when she made her first film. Naomi Watts was 36 when she got the lead role in *King Kong*. Kathryn Joosten, who gave such stunning performances in *Desperate Housewives* and *The West Wing*, did not even start acting until she was 42. Gerard Butler got his first role when he was 27 and only went to Hollywood when he was 30. Felicity Huffman only got an agent when she was 27. If you are 18 and reading this then do not get bitter and worried as the years go by. You are going to live for a very long time and you can tell stories at any age. Don't get discouraged by 'waiting for something to happen'. You never know how far away you are from success. It was Eddie Cantor who said it 'takes twenty years to become an overnight success', and it is true.

Of course you could actually never become famous but that does not mean you won't be a working actor with a great career.

How To Be A Successful Actor. Becoming an Actorpreneur.

And now for the positives. Acting is a wonderful career and if you have talent and you get some opportunities, you will be fine. Acting is an amazing profession and can also be surreal. In fact, nothing else quite compares to it. When you get that call saying you got the part it feels like winning the lottery. It is, without a doubt, the best feeling in the world. It is a high you never really come down from. Even when the part is done and dusted and you think back to that moment.

Acting gives you the kind of life dreams are made of. You will meet amazing people, go to amazing places. Everyday will be different and you never know exactly what will happen. At any moment your life could change and you could get that call that changes your entire life.

As an actor most of your life will be spent not doing what you have trained for. Most of it will be spent applying for jobs, auditioning, training, networking, administration and doing your tax. It is not for the work-shy.

There is no calling in sick in the film industry. It is just too expensive. Only death is a reasonable excuse not to turn up. Your death - not a loved one's. The show must always go on.

So - is it all worth it? The early mornings, cold days and anti-social hours. Absolutely.

Francis Ford Coppola said that 'making films is not fun'. In a way he is spot on. It's not coal-mining or brain surgery. Not many things are. But what makes it all worth it is the end result. Contributing to a piece of cinematic history. Seeing your work on the big screen - or small - is like no other feeling in the world.

Here are a few wonderful things I have learned in the course of my acting career so far.

How to stamp on the eighth Dr Who's head without hurting him

In 2010 I was cast as a seventeen-year-old thug. A complete stretch if you know me. I once had a part in the cult television series *Luther* in which I had to stamp on Paul McGann's head. Because Paul is such a big star - and a really nice guy who came down to talk to me and my fellow actors even though we are only there for a day, something that not all of the big stars do, I had to first meet up with the stunt coordinator so I didn't actually smack Paul in the face. Or worse. Kill him. So, at a brewery in East London I met up with the stunt coordinator. Who promptly accidentally hits me in the face when I try to get a better look. It hurts. I get the irony but I laugh it off. So, on set - keep out of the way of the stunt coordinator's elbows.

How not to embarrass yourself in front of Dustin Hoffman

The title is actually a lie. I did not manage this, I have met Dustin Hoffman a few times now and he is quite lovely. I was on a film set and I saw Dustin waving and smiling. I smiled and waved back. Only to realise that he was waving at the person behind me...I remain mortified to this day. He was nice about it though. I just did the whole British thing of pretending it never happened.

How to motivate an actor to push you down the stairs

How To Be A Successful Actor. Becoming an Actorpreneur.

On the set of *Zombie Apocalypse* I not only decapitated a zombie (lots of fun, done with special effects and precise spade movements) I had to throw a zombie down the stairs. This was obviously not a real zombie, it was a person and I didn't want to kill him. After two takes he was not feeling it. So, he said to me 'If you hurt me I will buy you a drink.' The next take the director got his shot and the zombie came up to me limping and says: 'I owe you a drink.' All is fair in love and film-making.

How to pickpocket

Filming can be boring. Incredibly so. It was while waiting around on a Poker star commercial (a shoot that was incredibly fun, mostly due to the amazing cast and crew) that I learned a rather old school trick that should help if the acting work ever dries up: how to pickpocket. Basically, you 'bump' into someone. Then you apologise. When you bump into them you swiftly grab their wallet out of their pocket. They are so distracted that they don't notice. Also they do not feel it as you hit them somewhere else. Genius!

Note: I don't recommend you try this and I take no responsibility for any problems or legal issues which may arise if you do.

Brian Moloko will show you how to put a drip in your hand

At Three Mills Studio in East London, with make-up that makes me look like a junkie, I met a childhood hero, Brian Moloko, and he showed me the correct way to put a drip in my hand. This was for the music video for the Placebo song, *For What It's Worth* (https://www.youtube.com/watch?v=RBeCgtgr6Rs). The music video did a lot of good for my career and has had over a million views on YouTube. Doubt I will use this skill but if a career in nursing ever beckons....

Right, now how to build up your future acting career.

Starting Out

Watch as much theatre and film as you can. If you cannot afford to go to the theatre or cinema then become a reviewer. There are plenty of sites out there looking for reviewers. You can also join sites like Show Films First (http://www.showfilmfirst.com/) or Masterclass (http://www.masterclass.org.uk/) If you live in London you will have to be quick though, these tend to go fast.

If you are under 25 there is plenty of free theatre available to you. If you live in a city then you have no excuse not to go to museums and art galleries. There is an entire world on your doorstep if you live in London so see as much as you can.

Watch films, take classes, get some friends together and practice scenes and talk about the industry. Think boy scouts: always be prepared. You can get an audition at any point. If you have not acted in six months then you might be more nervous at an important audition. It is better to stay ready than to get ready. Keep your instrument sharp.

Now let's get down to the nitty gritty: what are the basics you need for your new career? Here they are....

How To Be A Successful Actor. Becoming an Actorpreneur.

Actors today are lucky. In the past there were no such things as mobile phones and the internet. These two things have made an actor's life much easier. You don't have to stay at home and wait for your agent to ring (and you should never do that anyway) and you can market yourself through the internet and apply for castings via the many casting sites out there, most of which are relatively easy to join.

Before the joys of modern technology you had to do mail outs which cost a lot of money. A mail out is your headshot, resume and a covering letter sent in an A4 envelope along with a stamped addressed envelope. You would have to print out hundreds of headshots or go to a reproduction company. Both of which cost a lot of money. You would also need to have an answering machine, do rep (repertory theatre) and mostly rely on your agent.

Today's acting industry is vastly different, and much better for it. In a way it has made an actor's life easier, and in other ways it is harder, as the industry is now more oversubscribed than ever before. The competition is fierce and the pay is worse. There are so many actors that we are always replaceable. There will always be someone else who can do the job, and for less money. Do not be downbeat about this however, if you are right for the part it will belong to you and no one else. There are things you can do to make yourself indispensable.

As an actor in today's society your life and career are in your own hands. Be thankful of this. Here is what you need:

➢ A good headshot. I recommend Diego Indraccolo. He is amazing and does mine. Find him here: http://www.diego.indraccolo.com/

➢ A Spotlight entry. Essential. You are invisible without it.

➢ Join acting sites like Starnow, Casting Call Pro, Mandy.com, Shooting People, Casting Network and Castweb. http://www.uk.castingcallpro.com/view.php?uid=44261. Some of these are free and some cost a lot of money. I am on all of them and not only do I get jobs but I can also ask for advice and it gives me a sense of community. Essential for an actor as our job can be very isolating.

➢ A good, concise covering letter that says something about you and shows some personality. Make it interesting and tweak it for each job. Make sure there are no spelling or grammar mistakes.

➢ A good resume. Leave out damaging information like your age and put your playing range instead. Your playing range should be a ten-year range. Say twenty to thirty. Try not to lie. The industry is tiny and you will probably be caught out. Though actors do lie about their age. Jessica Chastain recently said that she is vague about her age as she can play any role, but in the age of IMDB and Wikipedia, lies always get found out. Quite a few famous actors have been caught lying about their age.

➢ Be proactive. Do your own work. If you do not seem to be getting work then write your own script. Just get out there and be seen.

➢ Networking. Do this as much as possible. Not just to get jobs but so you know people in the same business.

➢ Get an agent. Not easy but they can get you castings you will not be able to get yourself. It is

How To Be A Successful Actor. Becoming an Actorpreneur.

possible to have a career without one but you will need one eventually.

➢ Be well groomed at all times. You are a business. No one wants to work with an actor who cannot look after themselves. Also: be nice or you will probably never work again.

➢ Only act if you cannot do anything else. It is the hardest and most competitive industry you can go into. Your chances of success at making a full-time living for the rest of your life are small.

➢ Exercise. You need to be in shape. Not just to look good, but also because acting takes a lot of stamina and energy.

➢ A secure internet connection. An internet connection is a must and so is a smartphone. I know not everyone can afford a Blackberry or an iPhone but it is important that you do not miss a valuable casting or email that could change the course of your career. You will use the internet to apply for jobs, find the contact details of people in the industry and keep up on what is happening in the world of entertainment.

➢ You need a computer and a printer.

➢ You will need a good professional name. Make sure that Equity and Spotlight do not have anyone else with the same name. Equity does not allow two actors to have the same name. You will have to change your name if someone else already has it. Which will be annoying and possibly damaging if you have already started to build up your brand.

➢ You will have to register as self-employed within three months. Otherwise you will get fined.

➢ A good collection of clothes for auditions and networking. If you buy an item of clothing 'wholly and inclusively' for your business it is tax deductible. Try to buy clothes that suggest different eras and characters. You do not have to go overboard. Just buy a few key items like a suit.

➢ Equity membership. It validates you. You will get insurance and discounts. If someone does not pay you - which keeps happening to me! - they will sort it out for you. http://www.equity.org.uk/home//

➢ Don't be a jerk. Nobody wants to work with a jerk.

➢ Turn up, be on time, be professional. Know your lines. All of this matters. Work begets work. I always see someone I have previously worked with on jobs now.

➢ Have some audition speeches and songs to hand. Essential in case you get a last minute audition. Make sure that as you get older you are not still using the audition speech of a teenager. Know your type.

➢ Keep training. Learn different accents. Read plays. Do Pilates or yoga. You have to keep yourself in tip-top condition.

➢ Read as many plays and books as you can. If you are well-read it will show through.

➢ Join the youth theatre if you are young, some amateur dramatics if you are older.

➢ Take classes continuously. A good idea is to join the Actor's Centre. They have a wide variety of classes. (http://actorscentre.co.uk/)

➢ Consider going to a drama school. More information on UK drama schools at http:www.drama.ac.uk and http:www.ncdt.co.uk. More on drama schools in chapter two.

➢ Buy *Contacts*, which is an acting reference book which is updated every year. *Contacts* is from the same people who do Spotlight and can be bought at http://

How To Be A Successful Actor. Becoming an Actorpreneur.

www.contactshandbook.com/ for £12.99. It is a reference book for actors. It has the contact details for casting directors, directors, agents and many more industry people.

Chapter 2: Training. To Train or not to Train

To train or not to train. Well, it's a hard question. Actors who did not do the full three years training with one of the main accredited drama school used to be stigmatised and, to a degree, they still are.

I trained for one year at Motherwell College. I studied acting and performance. A lot of good actors have come from Motherwell College including Karen Bracken from *Being Human*. The most important thing that came from my acting course was the confidence I gained to get up on stage. When I went to audition for my course I had no idea what to do and had not prepared anything. I had wanted to do a different course and had already been offered a place to take art, but I heard they were auditioning for the drama course and I asked if I could audition.

They said yes and I went to the room where the hopeful people were waiting to audition. When it got to my turn I went into the room and I got up on stage and did an improvisation about how much I love my two brothers (soppy, I know) and after I had finished I heard the teachers who were holding the auditions say that I was talented and 'could definitely go far'. This was enough to give me a bit of confidence to go after my dream. Something I had not decided to do until that day.

I also joined the Youth Theatre. I have done courses run by the Royal Scottish Academy of Music and Drama, and the Old Vic. I did a workshop at the Old Vic which was run by the 'Old Vic: New Voices' people that was amazing. The actors running the course were very complimentary about my acting and it helped me a lot. I still get a warm glow thinking about it to this day.

However, I mostly learned on the job, and that is what I recommend. Controversial, I know. I have worked in casting and I can tell what drama schools people have come from a lot of the time. Acting is a natural talent, you can do it or you can't. You can learn to be a better actor, but if the talent is not there then it's not possible. It's a lot harder than it looks!

Film acting is another thing. Drama schools may make great theatre actors, but many of them cannot act on film. The problem is, they actually (obviously) *act*. They can be too shouty and sometimes don't seem to know where the camera is. There is an old adage that you should never be caught acting. Remember this! Overacting looks terrible, especially on camera, which tends to pick up every subtle movement.

I don't think training is essential, and I know many people in the industry will agree with me. Though probably not publicly. By 'training' I mean doing a full-time, three-year acting course. There is still quite a snobbish attitude towards people who do not train, but there is also a snobbish attitude to people who didn't train at the 'right' school. Some say this is because the accredited schools let employers know that you have been trained to the proper degree and that it is 'essential' to go to an accredited school, and that if you do not you cannot use your degree within the industry as employers do not trust it. I don't agree, but keep in mind that you will meet people who do think this way occasionally. I was at a party once and I was introduced to another actor. The person who introduced us said: 'I guess the most important question is what have you done, what shows have you been in?' the other actor replied, 'No, the important question is where did you train? That is much more interesting.' Quite condescending. The thing is, that actor had pretty much never worked, and I had worked a lot. Draw your own conclusions.

After saying all of that I do think that if you are going to do a three-year, full-time training course then do go to an accredited drama school. That way you will be making the most of your experience. It will cost a lot and take up a lot of time and you will not be able to work or audition while you are training. That is quite a commitment. There is no point in training at an out of the way drama school no one has heard of. When you go to RADA or Central you are paying for the 'brand name'. People see that on your resume and they are impressed and it will help you to get auditions. Another benefit of training at an accredited drama school is that you are automatically given Spotlight (and it is half price for the first two years) and Equity membership.

Contact the Conference of Drama Schools (CDS) or the National Council for Drama Training (NCDT) to find the best school for you. Don't apply to just one school, ask around. There is a list of accredited schools further down.

Different drama schools will have a different criteria for applying. You will probably have to pay a fee for auditioning. For audition speeches you will probably need one classic and one modern. Make sure the audition speeches are different from each other and show contrasting emotions (see more on audition speeches below).

You should apply to more than one school and make sure you choose the right course. It is best to apply a year before the course starts. Just contact the schools you are interested in and request a prospectus. All of the schools will also have a website which you should take a look at.

However, if you can get into RADA, do so. It is one of the most prestigious drama schools in the industry. Many famous actors went there including Gemma Atterton, Sir John Gielgud, Joan Collins, Glenda Jackson, Sir Anthony Hopkins, Alan Rickman and Lord Attenborough. It will help your career beyond words. RADA is a brand name and will get you auditions that other actors cannot get. You will also be more likely to get an agent. The same goes with Central, LAMDA, RSAMAD and the other accredited drama schools. You will also receive a nationally recognised qualification at these schools. Either a university degree or a national diploma

If you can't get into an accredited drama school, or you can't afford it, don't despair; it doesn't mean you can't become an actor. Working on the job is the most important thing, for some people training may not be worth it financially. I think it is possible to take some classes, do a year's training, or just learn on the job. You also won't be saddled with a lot of debt in a career that pays less now than it did fourteen years ago.

If you already have some drama experience you could be eligible to do a post-graduate or a two-year course. If you don't then you may have to do the full three years. The Conference of Drama Schools (CDS) represents all the major drama schools and they publish an annual official guide to vocational training.

If I was going to get a degree I would have got one in English Literature or Psychology, this will teach you about words and human behaviour: more useful for an actor than pretending to be an animal or a tree, which I actually did at drama school. Just because I don't recommend spending three years getting a degree in acting does not mean you should not take acting classes. Take classes in accents, auditions, acting and dance. These are important. Invest in your career, it will pay off. You are a business. The good news is that it is all tax deductible. As long as you register yourself as self-employed. Which you must do so within three months of becoming self-employed or you will get fined.

Becoming an actor is a brave move. Unlike other professions there is no clear cut way to get into the acting business. You can't just go to university and then when you leave you are an actor. It is a hard profession. It is hard to break into and hard to maintain a career. There is no best way in or promise of success. There are just over 40,000 actors in Spotlight in the United Kingdom alone. That is a lot of competition.

If you are reading this and you have just left drama school then you will probably spend the next ten years of your life on the audition circuit with varying degrees of success. Everyone thinks they will become rich and famous straight away, but the reality is very different. While it is possible to be a working actor becoming a movie star has the same odds as winning the lottery.

When I was training I got the speech that acting teachers always give their students, about unemployment, dropout rates, the chances of success. Like any proper actor I decided to ignore all of this and hold on to this gem instead, 'Shoot for the moon, the very least that will happen is that you will end up amongst the stars'. Indeed.

Funding

The main problem for most people will be funding. There are ways to fund your way through drama school.

If you are from a country in the European Union then contact department for Education and Skills EU Means Testing Team on 01325 391199.

If you have a disability then go to the Skill website. It contains funding information for disabled students. SKILL: National Bureau for Students with Disabilities. 0800 328 5050. www.skill.org.uk.

If you want to see a list of Accredited Drama Schools go to http://www.drama.ac.uk or The National Council for Drama Training (NCDT)

Some accredited drama schools and their details are below.

Bristol Old Vic Theatre School, 1-2 Downside Road, Clifton Bristol, bs8 2xf T: +44 (0) 117 973 3535 E: enquiries@oldvic.Ac.UK www.oldvic.ac.uk

Principal: Paul Rummer. Central School of Speech & Drama

Central School of Speech & Drama Eton Avenue, London, nw3 3hy T: +44 (0) 20 7722 8183 F: +44 (0) 20 7722 4132 E: enquiries@cssd.Ac.Uk www.cssd.ac.uk

 Principal: Gavin Henderson

How to apply For undergraduate courses, please apply through UCAS (the Universities and Colleges Admissions Service. www.ucas.ac.uk) using the specific course codes.

Cygnet training theatre

New Theatre Friars Gate, Exeter, Devon ex2 4az T: +44 (0) 1392 277189 F: +44 (0) 1392 277189 E: cygnetarts@btconnect.Com W: www.cygnetnewtheatre.com

Principal: Rosalind Williams

To apply please call +44 (0) 1392 277189 or visit our website www.cygnetnewtheatre.com

Drama Studio London

Grange Court, 1 Grange Road, London W5 5QN T: +44 (0) 20 8579 3897 F: +44 (0) 20 8566 2035 E: admin@ dramastudiolondon.Co.Uk www.dramastudiolondon.co.uk

Principal: Peter Craze

Selection for admission is made by audition, recall and personal interview with senior staff. We look solely for talent, maturity, and the potential to become a successful working actor. For an application form email admin@ dramastudiolondon.co.uk or visit www.Dramastudiolondon.co.uk

Drama Centre

10 Back Hill, London, EC1R 5EN T: +44 (0) 20 7514 7022 F: +44 (0) 20 7514 8777 E: drama@arts.Ac.Uk www.Csm.Arts.Ac.Uk/drama

Principal: Professor Vladimir Mirodan,

Admission to all courses is by audition and/or interview.

GSA - Guildford School of Acting

Stag Hill, Campus University of Surrey, Guildford gu2 7xh T: +44 (0) 1483 560701 F: +44 (0) 1483 684070 E: gsaenquiries@gsa.Surrey.ac.uk www.gsauk.org

Director: Peter Barlow

Apply directly to GSA. Applicants can download a prospectus/application form from our website: www.Gsauk.Org or email/ telephone us to request these: *Admissions Officer:* T: +44 (0) 1483 684052 E: gsaadmissions@ gsa.Surrey.ac.uk

Guildhall School of Music & Drama

Silk Street Barbican London, EC2Y 8DT T: +44 (0) 20 7382 2323 F: +44 (0) 20 7382 7207 E: drama@gsmd.Ac.Uk www.gsmd.ac.uk

Principal: Professor Barry Ife

Please apply directly to the School.

Mountview Academy of Theatre Arts

Ralph Richardson Memorial Studios, Kingfisher Place, Clarendon Road, Wood Green, London N22 6XF T: +44 (0) 20 8881 2201 F: +44 (0) 20 8829 0034 E: enquiries@mountview.org.uk www.Mountview.org.uk

Principal: Sue Robertson

To apply please contact Mountview direct.

Manchester School of Theatre

Manchester Metropolitan University, Mabel Tylecote Building, Cavendish Street, Manchester, M15

How To Be A Successful Actor. Becoming an Actorpreneur.

6BG T: +44 (0) 161 247 6969 E: courses@mmu.ac.uk www.theatre.mmu.ac.uk

Head of School of Theatre: Niamh Dowling

Apply online through UCAS www.ucas.com

The Oxford School of Drama

Sansomes Farm Studios, Woodstock, ox20 1er T: +44 (0) 1993 812883 F: +44 (0) 1993 811220 E: info@oxforddrama.ac.uk www.oxforddrama.ac.uk

Principal: George Peck

Apply directly to the School.

RADA - Royal Academy of Dramatic Art

62-64 Gower Street, London, wc1E 6ed T: +44 (0) 207 636 7076 F: +44 (0) 207 323 3865 E: enquiries@rada.Ac.Uk www.Rada.org

Director: Edward Kemp

Rose Bruford College of Theatre & Performance

Lamorbey Park, Burnt Oak Lane, Sidcup, Kent da15 9df T: +44 (0) 20 8308 2600 F: +44 (0) 20 8308 0542 E: enquiries@bruford.ac.uk www.Bruford.ac.uk

Principal: Professor Michael Earley

Apply through http://www.ucas.com where you will be able to apply online. UCAS Institution Code: rose R51

RSAMD - Royal Scottish Academy of Music And Drama

100 Renfrew Street, Glasgow, G2 3DB T: +44 (0) 141 332 4101 F: +44 (0) 141 332 8901 E: registry@rsamd.Ac.Uk W: www.Rsamd.Ac.Uk

Principal: Professor John Wallace OBE MA

Apply directly to the RSAMD: T: +44 (0) 141 270 8265 E: dramaadmissions@rsamd. ac.uk or danceadmissions@ rsamd.Ac.Uk www.Rsamd.ac.uk/academy/ how-to-apply

RWCMD - Royal Welsh College of Music & Drama

 Castle Grounds, Cathays Park, Cardiff, CF10 3ER T: +44 (0) 29 2039 1361 F: +44 (0) 29 2039 1301 E: admissions@rwcmd.ac.uk www.rwcmd.ac.uk

Principal: Hilary Boulding

Apply direct to RWCMD.

There is a lot of competition for places at Drama Schools, especially for the top schools so don't get disheartened if you don't get in on the first year. There are fewer than 1000 places within CDS drama schools. It takes some people years to get in. This is also the reason why you should apply to more than one school.

Auditions are generally held between November and April every year. Most drama schools also

14

charge people to audition. The fee is usually around £30. Make sure that you do your research before you apply to schools. Then make a list of the ones you want to go to. If you are unsure go to an open day, most schools have one. Try and have a look around the school and talk to previous students. Also find out what actors have studied there who later became successful.

The Audition.

Every school will have different audition requirements but usually you will be required to prepare two contrasting (different in emotion and tone) monologues. One modern and one classical. Everything from 1960 onwards is considered modern and before that is classical. Your classical speech will probably be from Shakespeare. You may also have to do a musical number if you are applying for a musical theatre course. Your speech should be between two to three minutes in length. You may also have to do some group improvisation as well as voice and dance workshops as part of the audition.

One of the most important things to remember at an audition is to hold your nerve. Everyone gets nervous, and as each audition costs you money, even more pressure is piled on. Don't worry if you get a bit flustered or forget a line; your performance is what is really important. You need to have an understanding of the character you are playing and the text. See more on how to prepare for auditions and dealing with nerves in the 'Auditions' chapter later.

If you are asked to do the speech differently it does not mean you were wrong, they just want to see if you can take direction. The best thing you can do is comes across as mature and intelligent, with an understanding of text.

If your audition is successful you may be asked to a callback. This means that they liked what you did and want to see more of you.

If you are an international student then you should contact the school you want to go to directly. Some schools hold auditions in other countries or will let you audition via a self-taped audition. You may be able to audition via Skype. It is worth asking. Be sure it is what you want to do though as you will not be able to apply for funding assistance and it will cost approximately £12,000 per year and you will have to pay your own living costs. Yikes.

Unfortunately there is still a lot of snobbery in acting and if you are going to train you really should train at one of these schools (see list above). They will get your career off to the best start.

Chapter 3: The Craft

I have always thought of acting as a kind of 'action writing'. Okay, to be honest I stole the 'action-writer' thing from Jack Nicholson. You are a storyteller who uses all of yourself to tell the story. An actor researches a role and then shows the audience what they have found.

It will help to be interested in psychology. When I was doing a drama course what I learned was that every single thing about a person tells you something about them. From the way they speak, to the way they hold themselves and the way they walk. Everyone's life is in their voice and their mannerisms. You must learn how to read people and your character. You have to get into your character's head and known them inside out. Otherwise you will not do justice to them or their story. You must know your character, their circumstances, the world around them and why they do what they do. There is a very good book on body language and human behaviour called *What EveryBody Is Saying* by Joe Navarro who is an ex-FBI agent. Read it and learn.

Angelina Jolie says, 'Acting is not pretending or lying. It's finding a side of yourself that's like the character and ignoring your other sides.' (Quote from http://en.wikiquote.org/wiki/Talk:Angelina_Jolie)

I have noted some acting methods below. Try to take a class on each and see which one is right for you. Maybe that will be none of them and you will come up with your own way to build your character. That's okay too. It does not matter how you play your character, just that you do it well. The most important thing about your acting technique is that no one can see it!

Meisner

The Meisner technique was developed by Stanford Meisner, an American theatre practitioner. Meisner worked with Lee Strasberg and Stella Adler and later devised his own acting technique. Meisner described acting as 'living truthfully under imaginary circumstances' and he devised a number of training exercises. These exercises build on one another and help the actor develop the ability to improvise and access their emotional life.

Tom Cruise, Steve McQueen, Jeff Bridges and Grace Kelly all trained in the Meisner technique

Stanislavski

The Stanislavski system was created by Constantin Stanislavski. It is based on the concept of emotional memory. It gets the actor to focus internally to portray their characters emotion. *An Actor Prepares* by Stanislavski is probably the most famous acting training book ever written and essential reading for all aspiring actors.

The Method

How To Be A Successful Actor. Becoming an Actorpreneur.

The Stanislavski Technique was influenced by the Method. The Method was devised by Lee Strasberg. With the Method technique actors draw on their own emotions and memories to play the character. It also teaches sense memory, when you take a specific memory from your own life which causes the required emotion needed for the scene. They taught this on my drama course. I do use it occasionally. Be careful when you do this: if an emotion is too traumatic it should not be used. Your mental health is important, much more important than any role. Make sure the memory is not one that is too recent or painful.

The Method is famously used by Al Pacino, Robert De Niro and Dustin Hoffman.

Do a Google search for classes in your area and try to find some of the many books on any of these techniques to see if they are for you.

Do not get too wrapped up in techniques, just do whatever works. One of my favourite acting stories is when Laurence Olivier and Dustin Hoffman were doing *Marathon Man* together. 'Try acting. . . It's much easier!' Olivier jokingly told Strasbergian Method actor Dustin Hoffman, after Hoffman deprived himself of sleep for two days preparing for the famous 'Is it safe?' scene.

Chapter 4: Getting Work

This is the hard bit.

Work for free on as many student films as you can. You can find this via Shooting People, Starnow, mandy.com or by contacting film schools. Also do fringe theatre. Find fringe theatre work by contacting theatres, and through casting websites like Casting Call Pro and the Equity Jobs Board. Put together a showreel from the student films and you will already be ahead of most actors. Although I don't agree with actors not being paid, when you are first starting out it is okay to work just for expenses so you can build up footage for a showreel, gain experience and make contacts. All through your career there will be options to work for free. If the production genuinely has no money or you love the script then it will probably be worth it if you are not doing anything else. I have worked for free on friends' projects in the past and it always leads to me meeting other people or getting paid work in the future.

The first thing you will need before you can start applying for auditions is a headshot. Headshots are expensive so ask around for a recommendation before you pay out hundreds of pounds. There are always photographers offering free headshot on Starnow in return for the experience and the use of the image afterwards. If you know a photographer then ask them for a favour. I wouldn't recommend doing your own head shots unless you are incredibly talented at photography. Always better to find someone else or save up for professional ones.

The most important thing about headshots is that they look like you. When I have cast projects in the past (I have dabbled in some other areas of the industry) I am always shocked at how little actors look like their photo. This will not help your career. If people hire you or call you in for an audition thinking you look exactly like your photo and you look completely different, they will feel cheated and will never call you in for an audition or work with you again.

I cast a music video just from photos a few years ago and when the models turned up the director and I were distraught to find that we did not recognise any of the models, and that they were completely wrong for the part. All of their photos had been airbrushed beyond recognition.

You have to know which roles you should be applying for so make a detailed assessment of who you are. Not what you want to be. Be honest with yourself.

Think about how you move, talk, stand and your physical appearance. Go head to toe. Think about your likes and dislikes. Think about your clothes, what is unique about you. Where you are from?, what accent do you have? You have to know who you are before you can tell other people. For example I have very pale skin and I tend to get cast in period roles. The acting industry is the only industry where it is okay to judge people on their physical appearance. And you will be. A lot. Also, if you look Italian but are English, you will probably be cast as Italian. Think of the Welsh Catherine Zeta Jones and how she made her name playing Spanish roles because of her black hair, brown eyes and olive complexion.

Sometimes where you are from can be a disadvantage. I am Scottish and was told by a director that the reason he had not hired me for any of his films was because he 'did not have any Scottish parts'. I have never actually played a 'Scottish part' in my life, but some of my characters did have Scottish accents, and some of them didn't.

Actors today are luckier than any actors of a past era. Why? The internet. Acting used to be a closed shop. Now anyone with an internet connection and a headshot can apply for a large number of castings every day. This may make it easier but it also means there are more actors than ever before. The competition is immense. Even for an unpaid role hundreds of people will apply, and for the big roles you will be up against thousands of people from all over the world. If you are lucky enough even to get the audition.

It is hard to say which one of these casting sites (see more below) is best as I think different sites have different success rates for different people. I recommend trying them all at least once. However, you must be on Spotlight. If you are not on Spotlight, you are invisible. Nothing will affect your career as badly as not being on Spotlight as most castings come through it and then you, or your agent, can submit you through 'the link'.

The best advice I can give you is to join Spotlight as soon as possible and PUT A SHOWREEL ON. It costs £31 on top of what you are already paying (£146 at time of going to press), but it will pay off. You will also not get an agent if you are not on Spotlight as they will not be able to put you forward for jobs. You need four professional credits to be on Spotlight or you need to have trained at an accredited drama school. However, it is hard to get these credits without being on Spotlight. It is a catch 22 but you will be able to get around it.

How To Get Those Four Credits

There are a few ways to get around this. If you decide to train then your drama school credits are allowed as long as they are from an accredited school. My school was not accredited but the credits were still accepted. It helps to be a little cheeky when you are starting out. You may have to be economical with the truth. Do some student or low budget films to get some credits. Fringe theatre can also help. Even featured extra work (emphasis on 'featured') can count. Remember: you only need four credits and as long as you follow the above advice then these are not that hard to get. If you really struggle to get four credits then make some short films or put on a play. Make up a pseudonym or juggle the credits of the people you make your projects with. For example: be the director on each other's credits. You have to have imagination, guts and a good work ethic to be a successful actor, nowhere is this more true than at the beginning. Technically your own project may not count as a 'professional' credit, but you are a professional making work so *all's fair.*

My first four credits were my college productions, a short film I acted in and a role I had on a television show called River City. Funnily enough, I got my (tiny) role in River City when I was an extra. An actress had not turned up and they needed a role filled. The director spotted me and another girl and asked us if we would like to audition for the part. We both obviously said yes. I won the part over her. This combination of luck and going for it is what makes an acting career. You have to work hard to get yourself opportunities and *then* you have to make those opportunities pay off. Seeing myself on national television for the first time was an experience I will never forget. My family were so proud. It spurred me on.

Back to casting sites. Other sites I have found that are good for work are Castweb, Starnow, Shooting People, Equity Job Board, PCR, IMDBpro, Castnet and Castingcallpro (See more details below). *The Stage* also has auditions in it. I have made a detailed assessment of all of these casting sites below, including costs.

You can find your own work through word of mouth. Use your contacts. You can also find work through Facebook and Twitter. Follow directors and casting directors on Twitter. Like them on Facebook too. You can find out about castings this way and also build up your network.

Mandy.com and Talent Circle are free and have the occasional great job. Join them.

All of this does add up but it is all tax deductible. If finance is tight then just be on Spotlight. Being an actor is an expensive business.

Ring theatres to find out what and when they are casting and do your research. Don't be scared to cold call and send emails to people. The Actor's Yearbook has a casting calendar which can be incredibly useful.

Register on all of the major quality casting sites and databases and keep everything updated. It is usually free to have a profile even if you cannot apply for jobs. Get a new headshot every year and keep your credits and skills updated. *This is important*. You do not want a casting director to go to your profile and not hire you because it looks like you have not worked for three years when you did a brilliant job a few months ago.

Daily habits to get into:

Do at least half an hour of research every day. Become part of the industry you are in. Know who people are, what is being cast and who is casting it. Always be ahead of your competition. This may all sound daunting, and it is, it is a full time job just to get an acting job, however, you only need one of those jobs to launch your career. It will get easier as you make contacts and get used to the industry. One role can be your break out and it can come at any point. It is completely within your grasp, if only you put the work in.

Sites in the USA
http://actorsaccess.com
http://sag.org/iactor-online-casting (Need SAG membership)
http://nowcasting.com
http://castingabout.com

Sites in Europe
http:e-talenta.eu
http:casting-network.de

How To Be A Successful Actor. Becoming an Actorpreneur.

Sites in Australia
http://showcast.com.au

Sites in the UK
http://spotlight.com
http://castingcallpro.com
http://castweb.co.uk
http://shootingpeople.org
http://starnow.com
http://mandy.com

I have given more detail below about the casting sites in the United Kingdom that I have used.
Prices are correct at time of going to press.

Casting Sites In The UK

Star Now. Starnow.com

I like Starnow. It used to just be for beginners but there are some really good castings on their site.
The people who run it are also nice. I got a part in Placebo's music video *For What It's Worth*
thanks to Starnow. It has had millions of views. I get recognised a lot from it. My Starnow profile
has also been viewed nearly 800,000 times.

Starnow does not charge you any more money for uploading pictures or videos so it is good value.
Some sites do. If you do well you can also become a pro member. This lets employers know that
you take your career seriously and makes sure that your applications go to the top.

I have an interview with Jessica Manins from Starnow in the Interview section.

£35.94 for 6 Months

Shooting people

Shooting People is amazing. Relatively cheap and a hubbub of film making. Lots of contacts to be
made here. They also do a monthly meet up. A lot of the castings are unpaid but you will be in
contact with the next Spielberg or Scorsese. It has a good community and some good castings. You
can also put up your showreel and films. You can then share them with other film makers. Well
worth it and affordable.

£30 per year but you can usually get a discount. Search for one online if times are tough.

Spotlight.

Every actor from Judi Dench to a new graduate is on Spotlight. The first piece of advice I got from
a casting director (Francesca Greene who was kind enough to call me at home when I was eighteen
and give me some valuable advice) was that you must be on Spotlight if you want to be an actor,

because if you are not you are invisible.

Your Spotlight page is available to anyone who has your link and by casting professionals with

access to the site. Spotlight also publishes an annual book of all of the actors in its database. Spotlight has changed over the years and it now has castings that actors can apply for directly. In the past, only agents could apply to the jobs on the site. In the acting world these jobs are called breakdowns. However the jobs you'll be able to see and apply for still won't be as good as the ones your agent gets.

Casting directors can filter who sees their castings or 'breakdowns'. If it is a big role they will probably only see a handful of people and possibly also only actors from a specific agency, like one of the top agents such as the Independent Talent Group. It's not fair but it is a fact of the business.

If you have an agent they will probably apply for these castings for you. Your agent can change your settings so that you can apply for castings yourself or you can 'nudge' them to let them know you want to be seen for a specific casting.

If you do not have an agent you can also list Spotlight as your point of contact. Which will help with any crazy people. You will also get a Spotlight card that offers a range of discounts.

To be on Spotlight you need four professional credits or to have trained at an accredited drama school.

Spotlight also do events and give career advice to actors. I interviewed Emma Dyson from Spotlight for this book. The interview has some really good information. Check it out in the interview section.

£146 for one year for Actors and Actresses.

PCR - Production and Casting Report.

Every actor has had PCR at some point in their life. It used to have the hold over Spotlight and be an essential. A rite of passage. Again, your agent will get this delivered to them. It is posted to you and then you search through the listings of new film, television and theatre projects and post off your resume and headshot or email, depending on the casting directors preference, for any projects you are interested in to the casting director. It comes on red paper (so it can't be copied) and a lot of the castings will not be happening for a while, but it is great for keeping up with what is happening in the industry. It is also great for building up a black book of contacts. If you can afford it, get it.

£22.46 per month

Casting Call Pro

Casting Call Pro is very easy to use. You just build your profile and then you can apply directly for castings. Your agent can also put you forward for castings. There is a free basic membership. With the free basic membership you can only apply for unpaid work.

It does get some good jobs. A few of my friends earn a lot of money from Casting Call Pro. About 60% of their income.

There have been some grumbles about the fact you can't just put a playing range, you have to put a specific year and then if the casting is outside of this age range you will not be able to apply for that role. Even if it is only by one year. Here is what Casting Call Pro say about it on their website:

'As an actor on Casting Call Pro you will be able to set your playing age to the age you feel best

represents your looks. Playing age can be set independent of your actual age. It will then be used by casting directors to limit searches and used to ensure only appropriate actors can apply for roles listed on the jobs board.

'For the majority of actors, your playing age will be similar to your actual age. For those actors who tend to be cast in roles younger or older than your actual age, adjust accordingly.

'If you are used to using an age range, simply select the midpoint of your age range as your playing age.

'Once you have set your playing age you'll be able to apply for any castings where your playing age falls within the playing age range set by the casting director. If your playing age is outside the range set by the employer you'll be unable to apply, even if you fall outside just by one year.

'Given the opportunity over 80% of actors specify the maximum allowed age range - and in systems which sometimes allow very broad age parameters, as wide as twenty years. This results in actors saying they can play 25 or 45, or 16-30. While the broad age range is very attractive to the actor, we believe this is unrealistic - a 16 year old doesn't look like a 30 year old, nor does a 25 year old look like a 45 year old! As such we ask actors to provide us with a single playing age around which casting directors can make age-range based judgements.'

I don't agree but apart from that, I don't have any complaints. It is a good site with some good castings.

It also has a forum that is good to connect with other actors and ask any questions. Casting Call Pro also has a resource section which has the details of photographers and other services.

I interviewed Simon Dale from Casting Call Pro. You can find the interview in the interview section.

£117.50 a year for a premium membership, Also offers a free basic membership.

Castweb

Castweb is different from the other services as you get emails about castings or 'breakdowns' as we call them, and then you email the casting director your CV and headshot. It is mostly for agents but I have had a lot of luck with it. It is quite expensive. However, one good job will pay that off. If you can afford it, get it. Your agent will already have it. So ask them if it is needed if money is very tight.

£139.95 for 12 Months

Mandy.com

How To Be A Successful Actor. Becoming an Actorpreneur.

This site is completely free and gets the occasional good casting. Definitely worth it.

Free

Talent Circle

This is also free and has occasional good paying jobs. At the beginning of my career I got some

very good jobs from it.

To sum up ...

As you no doubt noticed all of these casting sites cost quite a bit of money. I told you acting was not cheap. Unfortunately to not be on these sites is a false economy. You just have to book one job and then that will pay for an entire year's membership.

There are also a number of blogs out there that can be invaluable. Google these and have a read: http://thedailyactor.com, Bonnie Gillespie's blog The Actor's Voice (I have read Bonnie's books on acting and they are really good. Especially *Getting Down To Showbusiness*), http://showfax.com, Backstage Magazine, Playbill, The Film Set on Frost Magazine (sorry, being biased, this is my online magazine) and http://actorcastblog.com.

Also make sure you read the trade magazines like PCR, Variety, Hollywood Reporter and Screen International to know what is happening. Also use http://IMDBpro.com. You need to know what is in preproduction and what is being cast. Find out if there are roles in the project that you could play, and then send an application. Make sure there is a role appropriate for you: you do not want to annoy casting directors by sending them useless emails. They will probably stop reading them and if a role comes along that you could have played you will lose out.

You can also do a self-tape audition. These have become very big as casting has become global. When a big film or television show is being cast they will probably audition actors in all of the major cities: LA, New York, London, Glasgow and Sydney.

The major casting databases that casting directors use:

E-Talenta in Europe (outside UK)
Spotlight in UK
Breakdown services in US
Showcase and IACD in Australia.

Making Your Own Films to Promote Yourself.

You may wonder why this is here. You are an actor why would you make your own films? Well, think about this: Ben Affleck and Matt Damon were movie extras before they sold *Good Will Hunting* to Castle Rock Entertainment for $675,000 in 1994. They cast themselves, won an Oscar and are now two of the most successful actors in Hollywood. Sylvester Stallone did the same thing with *Rocky*. He wrote the script and refused to let anyone make it unless he was cast as the lead. It is now a classic film and he is one of the most successful movie stars of all time.

While you are applying for every job you can, buy a camera and make your own films and then put them on YouTube. Make your own Hollywood. Show people what you can do. I have a Canon 60D. It is a stills camera but the quality is so good you can make cinema quality films with it. It was expensive but you can buy a cheaper one, like a Flip Camera. I have had lots of jobs just from my showreel. You have to get your face out there.

I made a comedy web series with some friends called *Love Tourettes*. We just made it with whatever equipment we had to hand. I still get recognised from it to this day in castings and also by random people. People even ask when we will do more and it has had thousands of views. I have also made some short films and also co-wrote/directed/produced and starred in a feature film called *Prose & Cons*. Which also features Bo Wilson who I made *Love Tourettes* with, Lynn Howes who starred in it and some other amazing actors.

I started a film production company with someone I met on a film set called Steve McAleavy and I can now make the projects I want and not wait to be cast in things. I have surrounded myself with amazingly talented people like Jason Croot (who went to school with Steve and through whom I met Steve) who is an actor, producer and director. Jason casts me in his films and I cast him in mine. You will find this as your career progresses: you will work with a select bunch of people over and over again. I got very lucky to meet the talented actors, producers, writers and directors I have met. My career would be pretty lacklustre without them.

People will keep hiring you if you are reliable, easy to work with and you do a good job. It's a numbers job. Be seen to be working.

Get into the good habit of applying for castings every morning. There are a lot of sites out there and it will pay to go through them all.

Keep in touch with your agent. Let them know if you are going on holiday so they don't put you up for an audition you cannot go to. This will damage your reputation in the industry.

If you are a member of Equity they have an Equity Job Information Board. They now also email castings to you which I find very handy.

Always check your messages and your emails. Respond to messages immediately and do not let people down. Reputation is everything in this industry. If you let people down they will not hire you again. Sometimes people will call around for recommendations before they hire you. So be a good person, be professional and be on time.

Age

Age is always a sensitive issue. No more so than in the acting industry. Especially when you're playing age and real age can be very different. I remember playing a sixteen-year-old when I was twenty-three. All of the other actors, who were actually sixteen, thought I was old. It was quite amusing. I am in my twenties and quite often get cast as teenagers. I think age should work on a 'don't ask, don't tell' policy. In acting it is all about how you look.

I asked some acting friends on Twitter if they have ever lied about their age:

Emma Gable @emmagable
@**Balavage** I use playing age not real age - my real age not helpful for casting as it is quite different. But would always disclose if asked

Miss L @ProResting
@**Balavage** don't think I've ever had to. Would never put it on my CV though...

Actors Talk Podcast @actorstalk
@**Balavage** when I was younger I did cause I was cast younger than my age. Learned early not to give my real age. Not now. #**oldfart**

Lenka Silhanova @LenkaSilhanova
@**Balavage** I don't lie about my age, my playing age is closely around my age, too. However I only put playing age on my resumé.

Angela Peters @angiepang
Ditto! Age is but a number. but in this industry everyone does seem to care about that number. Best keep them in suspense @**Balavage** @**LenkaSilhanova**

Tony Ramos Nope. Never lie about my age because in the end, 'they' decide what age (range) I look like anyway. Still, it seems the people/actors that care about not revealing their age, are usually my lady actor lady friends.

Jack Bowman: No, I just don't tell people how old I am. Frazer Hines taught me the mantra - 'no wages, no ages'. Either you look the part, or don't.

The truth is, your real age can hurt your career and it can also enhance it. You just never know.

A lot of the actors I am the same age as and started out with are now five years younger than me! I don't think you should lie about your age. My advice it to be vague and tell everyone your playing age instead. Whether that be younger or older. The best person to tell your real age to is the casting director. They can then always lie to the director for you.

Emailing People.

You should have an email contact list. Keep people updated on what you are doing. Don't spam or bombard people and if they ask to be removed from any mailing list then do not be offended. It is best to email people individually. I do this. I once emailed over 400 casting directors personally in one week. It was exhausting and tedious but this is the type of thing you have to do for your career.

Email casting directors every nine months or if you have done something worth noting, like a play or a part in a TV show. Make sure you are not wasting their time and actually have something to say.

How To Be A Successful Actor. Becoming an Actorpreneur.

Marketing (See PR and Marketing Chapter for More)

Marketing yourself is very important. Have a website and update it. Even if it is a free blog from wordpress.com or blogger.com. Update your Spotlight and other casting sites. Have a Twitter and Facebook presence. Have a Facebook fan page that people can like and keep it updated with news and photos. Have a Twitter account for your acting and include you website or IMDB link in the biography. Tweet about acting and your career, but be very careful about tweeting about hangovers or anything negative. This will win you no fans and could even cost you a job.

Keep your social media presence out there. Tweet often and update your Facebook page regularly. Start a blog and write about your career. Make your own projects and update your showreel. Learn how to write a press release and when you are doing something of note, email the editors of newspapers and blogs. If you are doing theatre then it is worth paying for some flyers to distribute.

Always have your business card handy and take your headshot and a print out of your resume to auditions. Preparation is everything.

Chapter 5: Agents

It is not easy to get an agent. There are so many actors and thousands more graduate each year. Agents, even the bad ones, are simply inundated. The best way to get an agent is through word of mouth. Getting someone to recommend you to their agent is the quickest and easiest way in. Or you can do it the way I did it: I emailed, wrote to and phoned every agent in *Contacts* (a book published every year from Spotlight which has agents' and casting directors' details in) until I got an agent. It took a long time, about a year. My first agent wasn't very good, nor was the second one. But the agent I have now is amazing and that's how the acting game works. You build up your career brick by brick.

So, work through contacts, emailing or writing to every agent asking for an interview or audition or invite them to something you are in. Do this until you get an agent. Give your agent six months, if in that time they have not gotten you anything, email them and ask them if they think you should get new headshots, or just meet up for a talk. You don't need an agent to get work, but it's hard and almost impossible to get an audition for major television and film without one.

The internet is an amazing thing. You can find the details for practically every agent. You can also find out who represents people through IMDBpro or Who Represents: http://whorepresents.com. IMDBpro is something I think every actor should invest in. It is very helpful to have to hand.

Ask people for agent recommendations. Before you sign anything research the agent and always read the contract! Never sign anything without reading it first and ask for a copy. Most agents will want to sign you for a year and will also want advanced notice of a termination in the contract. The termination notice is usually a month.

Rule out the ones that are not for you, do your research, it is a small industry so don't embarrass yourself for applying for an agent that only does teenagers if you are 34.

Don't be scared to ask them about commission, contacts, what kind of work they would put you forward for and how long they have been in business.

Commission is usually between 10-20%. Be wary of agencies that charge more than this and run away from any agencies that want to charge you a fee. They are legally not allowed to charge a fee to join and are probably not legit.

The good news is that you do not need to have an agent to get work, or to be successful, but you are unlikely to make it big without one.

If you are freelancing and not signed exclusively with one agent then make sure you inform your agent when you secure work or an audition on your own or through another agent.

Your agent will put you forward for roles. They will also give you advice.

Your relationship with your agent

It goes without saying that your relationship with your agent is very important. You should check in with them and always let them know about any changes in your appearance. Also let them know about holidays and keep them updated on any work you do.

Never criticise your agent. Especially in public. It reflects badly on you and could get back to them.

If you don't feel like you are getting any auditions it may not necessarily be your agent's fault. Actors can go in and out of fashion. If you do think your agent is not really working for you, then just have a professional and honest chat with them. Sort out any problems immediately.

If you want to leave your agent, do so in an amicable way. Don't badmouth them to other people in the industry. Professionalism goes a long way.

Extra work and Extra Agencies

Extra work can be controversial. The jury is still out on whether people in the industry judge actors who do it. Some casting directors, like John Hubbard, actively encourage it. There is nothing wrong with doing it to get some experience and to pay the rent. Don't let anyone judge you or make you feel bad. Extra work will not improve your acting career but it will let you see how the industry works and will let you earn some good money. You will also make some friends.

If you really want to do it, do it for a year, two maximum, under a different name just to gain some experience of being on-set. However, it is best to only do extra work if you will be either deep background (and be aware that you will treated horrendously) or if you have a line and are featured, called a 'special' or "walk on'.

Extra agencies to join

Ray Knight
2020
Casting Collective
Mad Dog Casting

Stay in touch with people. As you build up your career you will find that most of your work probably comes from the same sources. Directors who enjoyed working with you and liked the job you did will re-hire you.

When you get a job or have a screening send an email to your contacts keeping them in touch, or inviting them to your screening or new show. Be in people's minds. If you are out of sight you will probably also be out of people's mind.

Double check your resume for spelling and grammar errors. You must look as professional as possible. Include your contact details or your agent's contact details. You must always be contactable. Google yourself: if you cannot find yourself, neither will casting directors.

How To Be A Successful Actor. Becoming an Actorpreneur.

Reputation is important and so is image. Make sure you keep both of these in pristine condition.

Chapter 6: Auditions

The first thing to do for your audition is turn up. Yes, really, there are actors out there who don't turn up to auditions, lots actually. Which is madness as they are so hard to get. So if you turn up you are already ahead of the game. Secondly, you should also be proud of yourself. It is incredibly hard to even get auditions. It is a compliment to get one and it means that people believe in you. So don't let them down.

You have to learn to love auditions because if you hate auditions then you will hate being an actor. Everyone has to audition. Daniel Craig had to audition for his part in the James Bond franchise and Anne Hathaway had to audition for her role in *The Dark Knight Rises*. Take comfort in the fact that even big stars have to audition.

If you are lucky you will audition a lot. Wentworth Miller from *Prison Break* had this nugget to say about auditions: 'You might look at my CV and see I've had 12 jobs, but I've been to over 450 auditions so I've heard "no" a lot more than I've heard "yes". So if I go in looking only to meet my own standards, then that will make taking that rejection a little bit easier. And when I do get that job it will seem like icing on the cake.' (Quote from Contact Music: http://www.contactmusic.com/news-article/wentworth-miller.-i.m-no-overnight-success)

Auditions are hard. They are nerve-wracking but they are your job. This is why the best thing you could do for your career is learn to love auditions. It is hard I know. Auditions are essential to your career and becoming good at them is the way you will book work. Just think of it as performing to the casting director your interpretation of the character. If you look at an audition as a chance to perform and tell a story it will be less painful.

For your audition learn the lines and be off book. This is important. Dress to suggest the character. When Alexandra Roach auditioned to play the young Margaret Thatcher in The Iron Lady she went in dressed as Margaret Thatcher and went to the hairdresser that morning to get her hair done just like Thatcher's. She booked the role and now has an amazing career.

Arrive early. If you are on time to an audition then you are already late. Hold your nerves. If it comes between you and another actor then the job will go to the person who can handle their nerves.

Doing a monologue for a drama school audition, theatre or an agent.

Go through your audition piece, think about the character, know them as much as you can.

With your audition speech remember to cast yourself intelligently. Find a role you can actually play that is within your age range and is in a dialect that you can do. Keep it short, two to three minutes maximum. Try not to do anything that is overdone. No Violas, Macbeths or Ophelia. Shakespeare is very overused. The audition panel will have heard it before.

You can write your own monologue if you want but make sure it is good enough. Ask a friend who will tell you the truth for their opinion.

Make sure you really warm up before your theatre audition. Warm up your voice and do some stretching. Make sure you do a monologue that you have practised enough. Go in with confidence and show them what you can do.

When you finish your monologue stay in character for a few seconds and then go back to normal. Give it a finish. It will make you stick in people's minds.

Research the director, the casting director and anyone else involved in the project. Watch their work and get the tone of it. Be as prepared as you can. This will give you an edge on your competition. If there is a scene then learn it.

Take a cold reading class as this will build up your skills. A cold reading is when someone hands you a script you have never seen before and you perform it without any preparation.

Decide what your character wants, what are their motives? Hold these intentions in your mind. Always know what your character wants. Take your time in the audition. Own the space. This is your time to show the casting director your interpretation of the character and how talented you are. Don't rush because you are nervous and want it to be over and done with. Stay as calm as possible. Show them what you can do.

Try not to think about how much you want or need the job. Desperation is never good and it will stop you from getting a part. It's important to try and have a little money stashed away to avoid this. It also means if there's a job you really don't want to do you don't have to take it.

Treat casting directors as human beings and don't be scared to ask them any questions.

What Happens at an Audition

Auditions are terrifying. Let's just get that bit over with. Everyone gets nervous. That is normal. You just have to handle your nerves and do the best you can do. Try anything that works, like meditation. Or breathing in for four and then out for four.

Learn any scenes before you go to your audition. Be off book if possible and make sure you have practised the accent enough. Research all of the people involved in the casting and be prepared.

The first thing to do when you go to an audition is arrive early. Thirty minutes is good. You will also want to prepare and be calm. Auditions are stressful and you want to compose yourself. Do not read a newspaper in the waiting room. Focus on your audition instead. Some casting directors have said that they hate it when they see actors reading papers instead of focusing on their audition. Don't let other actors distract you either. Focus.

Scan ahead when you are reading the script so you know what is coming. When you arrive you will have to fill in a form, you will then have your photo taken and wait to be seen. They will usually ask you your measurements, contact details, age and agent info. Have this info to hand. Don't lie about your age on the audition form but if you are uncomfortable then put an age range. Lying about your age can hurt sometimes. You have to be over twenty-five to do alcohol commercials.

When you go into the audition room there will probably be two or three people there. Possible people in the audition room are: the casting director, casting assistant, the director, a representative from an advertising agency and the producer. Treat each person equally. Even the receptionist when you come in. You never know who people actually are and whether they talk or not. People move jobs a lot and you don't know who the next big casting director or producer will be. Usually it will just be the casting director and an assistant though.

You will be asked to stand on a mark (usually an X marked in tape) and then you will face the camera and they will get a body shot, you will then move from left to right for a profile shot. You will then give your name to camera and the part you are auditioning for. You may also have to give your age and who your agent is. You will then go into the scene or monologue.

In the audition the casting director may ask you to do things differently even if they liked what you did just to see if you can take direction. It is important that you learn how to take direction well. The director will be able to see the entire film but you will only see things through the eyes of your character.

After you have finished, smile and say thank you. Shake people's hands and say goodbye. Leave quickly, don't loiter.

If you forget your lines DO NOT PANIC. The casting director will be understanding when it comes to some nerves. Just carry on as best you can.

Your audition will probably last a matter of minutes and then you are done.

Tip: Don't hyperventilate on camera to pretend you are crying, it doesn't work.

For commercial auditions you will probably just go in and have your picture taken. Commercial auditions are in, smile, out. Smile naturally. It is based on looks, if you look right, you will get the part. Other times you will do a quick scene with some other actors. They are usually easy and less stressful than film auditions when you have to learn seven pages of script off by heart. Commercials are still quite lucrative, though less so than in previous years. A good buyout will probably pay £3000 and £300 for the day. Avoid the word I, when auditioning for a commercial if you have to improvise; it is the project you are selling, not yourself.

When it comes to auditions there are a few important factors that will decide whether you get the job or not.

1)   Having the right look.

2)   Your talent

3)   Your professionalism and reputation

4)   Whether you can play the character.

How To Be A Successful Actor. Becoming an Actorpreneur.

After the audition forget about it. It is out of your hands and overanalysing and getting depressed won't help. Move on to the next opportunity. Auditions are hard and nerve-wracking so be proud of yourself for getting the audition and for having the courage to stand up in front of people to be judged. Be proud of yourself for following your dream.

It is normal to be nervous, but look at an audition as a chance to perform. There is no such thing as a wasted audition, once a casting director has auditioned you there is always the chance they will remember you and bring you in again.

Unfortunately they don't tell you if you haven't got the part, only if you have. And you can wait for months to hear anything even if you do get the part. I was basically told I got a part in a major BBC television show, and then waited for months for them to confirm until I finally got the picture. It's pretty rough but you just have to dust yourself off and move on to the next thing.

Approach the audition as if you already have the part and it is the first day of rehearsal. Give it your all and then forget about it. I know that can be hard. I have been upset about not getting a part. I went to the London Film Festival in 2012 and saw a film called 'Shell'. I had auditioned for the lead and not got it. The lead actress was also my casting 'type'. So she looked a little like me but also didn't. It was a very weird, surreal experience. The part just was not meant for me. I understood that and I got another job anyway.

Callback

Congratulations! You got a callback. They obviously liked you.

Relax, if you get a callback, they already think you are a good actor. You want to repeat what you did last time as much as possible. Wear the same thing if you can and replicate your previous audition. Make sure you take direction well. You are one step closer to your dream job.

The pressure will be ramped up but they already know you can act. Just go in the room and show them how right you are for the part. Then forget about it. You do not want to stress yourself out. I know it is hard but move on. If the part is right for you, you will get it. If it is not right for you then it just was not meant to be.

I asked Amy Hubbard of Hubbard Casting if I could print the following advice after she put it on the Hubbard Casting Facebook Group. Amy, and her family, are some of the most successful casting directors in the United Kingdom. They have cast some of the most successful films in history, including *The Lord of The Rings.* Amy has also been nominated for an Emmy, so she knows what she is talking about. Enjoy the advice and make sure that you like the group on Facebook. (https://www.facebook.com/groups/HubbardCasting/?fref=ts)

'For 99% of castings we use Spotlight - the industry leader for UK breakdowns. Facebook and Twitter are playing crucial role in our process when we need to spread the word or locate somebody. On my recent Irish commercial session, the final cast members were found via the following methods:

SUGGESTED BY AGENT - 6

34

How To Be A Successful Actor. Becoming an Actorpreneur.

SELF-SUGGESTED AFTER FACEBOOK POST / TWEET - 4
GOING TO DUBLIN COMEDY GIGS - 2
CAST IN PREVIOUS PROJECT - 1
SURFING NET - 1
RANDOMLY GOT IN TOUCH & WAS RIGHT FOR ADVERT - 1'

Amy went on to give this advice: 'During my marathon generals in Dublin this week one of the more common complaints was that it's difficult to get feedback; casters and possibly agents shy away from this INCREASINGLY as sometimes constructive criticism can be met with aggression. but here are some notes I made during the casting about how to improve advert auditions.

1: Eye lines: Make a plan before you come in. What is appropriate to the scene? Fixed point in the distance? Don't look at the ad agency / director: same as acting to camera this is breaking the fourth wall (the fourth wall is the audience. Never break the fourth wall or acknowledge the audience unless that is part of the script. It is the height of bad acting). Be aware of camera & position your body accordingly. but don't look at the camera unless you are identing (Identing is where you state your name, agent, age and the part you are auditioning for straight to camera before the audition starts) or asked to during the scene, but find a real fixed point.

2: Make a plan about your character. What are you wearing? Did you get the treatment and the script and DID YOU READ IT? Beyond that when the director opens his/her mouth LISTEN to the sequence you should follow. Like a sequence of steps.

3: Give it a finish. Don't relax when you've finished your bit, Stay in character until director has started talking (unlikely that you will hear 'cut') but hold it until you are sure scene is over. So many just relax physically and mentally 0.1 seconds after their last word or action. HOLD IT.

4: Caps for this one. DID YOU WATCH THE DIRECTOR'S PREVIOUS ADS to get onto his/her wavelength? Because I sure did.

5: Get there early. You may well be seen early, and you may well pick up extra knowledge. And if it's MY session I rarely 'cram them in' as I precast for all ads.

6: Work with your fellow actors. Apart from when the director is talking, they are the only people that matter in the room in terms of getting cast. If there is opportunity, of course acknowledge the caster and the cameraman, but we will understand if you don't. We will see you next time.'

I then asked Amy what the best way to be seen by a casting director was, and this is what she said: I would write to casters a maximum of four times per year with pertinent detail / recent changes.'

So there you go.

Accents

You should have a number of accents under your belt. If you learn one then it is usually just a case of brushing up when you have to use it again. When I first had to do an American accent for an

audition I drilled and recorded for hours every day. (Drill and record is when you listen to the

How To Be A Successful Actor. Becoming an Actorpreneur.

accent, copy it endlessly and record yourself to perfect it) Now I can slip into it when I need to.

Try *Accents: A Manual for Actors* by Robert Blumenfield and *A Course in Accent Reduction* by David Allen Stern.

When it comes to accents think of the ones that will be most useful to you. Only list accents that you have mastered on your Spotlight and your resume, get a native to help or a hire a dialect coach.

If an audition requires an accent do whatever you can to learn it: rent a film or listen to a radio programme or YouTube. If you can't do it, be honest and then say you will learn it.

When it comes to accents all casting directors and directors are different. Some casting directors prefer people to go in with the accent. Others prefer you to go into the accent when you start the scene. Try and research the specific casting director's preference. If you cannot find the information then you can always get your agent to ask the casting director before your audition. Or just ask them when you get there.

Penny Dyer has a good range of CDs called *Access Accents* which come with a booklet. I have her American Standard and her RP (Received Pronunciation) CDs. They are one hour long voice coaching sessions. I find them useful before an audition. You can also watch films and television shows to pick up an accent. The main thing is practice. Keep working on your skills just incase you get a last-minute casting for a specific accent.

Self-audition tape

Preparing for a self-audition.

One of the best things you could do for your acting career is invest in a camera (and you can get some very good cameras cheaply now). A separate microphone will also help. A lot of actors have booked amazing parts in films by recording themselves and sending their self-taped audition to the director and casting director. Casting is a global business now.

To do a self-taped audition you do not need the best equipment or lots of lighting. In fact, Benedict Cumberbatch got a part in *Star Trek* after filming his audition on his iPhone and Elijah Wood got his part in *The Lord of The Rings* after sending a self-taped audition to the casting director. The acting game has been changed and now everyone can take part. This does mean that there is more competition however.

If you can invest in a tripod, do so. You can get a cheap one and it's worth it because there are few things worse than a shaky camera. Try and get a friend to read the other lines and work the camera. The best way to do a self tape audition is to get a friend to help but if you invest in a tripod you can do them yourself. Line up the shot and do the scene a number of times. Get comfortable with the dialogue. Try to light yourself well. Even if you have to use a lamp or film near the window. If it is very quiet you could film outside, though if you film outside watch out for background noise.

Introduce yourself on camera and then say what part you are reading for. Make sure you also include your contact details. Keep it short. Feel free to talk about the character. Make sure you show passion. Keep everything to two minutes maximum.

When you are doing a self-taped audition make sure the focus is on you, not the other actor. You don't want your friend getting the job!

If filming with a scene partner, have them read their lines off camera. You don't want to confuse things. Keep the focus on you.

Get into character. The good thing about a self-taped audition is that there is less pressure and you can do as many re-takes as you want.

Do a medium shot and a close up.

Light it properly. Natural lighting can work. If not use anything you have to hand. Even a lamp or a torch will do.

Make sure you are listening, and listen well. A large portion of film acting is listening and not speaking.

Line your shot up properly; don't have too much wall behind you, or loud curtains. Think neutral.

Mic yourself properly by making sure the microphone can hear you properly and is not picking up any background noise. Film indoors if you live in a noisy area.

You have to play the character's needs. Don't play happy or sad, play the need and the emotion will come with it.

Every actor has a leading eye. Find out which one is yours and cheat it towards the camera.

Keep it simple with no blocking. Just focus the camera on you and act the scene. Don't do anything fancy.

Start with a wide shot that shows your entire body, do your profiles and then zoom in for an introduction. State your name, height and agent. Do not announce your age. If you are filming on your own then do your introduction, then cut and do your close up separately and then edit the two shots together.

Don't send the self-tape if it is not good enough. It will come back to haunt you.

Don't do too many takes, two maximum and if you send both takes to the casting director then make sure they are different.

Even if you are not doing a self-taped audition it is very important to film yourself. Find your flaws and bad habits. Practice, work hard and never stop studying your craft, you are battling in an ultra-competitive area.

Casting Notebook in North America, Spotlight in the UK and Breakdown Services all let actors put

How To Be A Successful Actor. Becoming an Actorpreneur.

themselves on tape. Http://castit.com is a good site that invites actors to audition for projects.

Self-tape auditions are getting more and more popular. Vera Farmiga got her part in Martin Scorsese's The Departed after making her own self taped audition and sending it to Scorsese.

There are over 40,000 actors in the UK, over half of whom live in London. There are more females, but fewer roles for females. Female roles are also usually written for young females, so the odds go down even further the older a woman gets, but so does the competition. Not fair but a stark reality.

Enjoy the casting. Prepare and make choices, act and react in the moment. Play the part in your eyes and possess an inner monologue, commit to the scene, stake a claim on the role and take a risk, Tell the story, but listen.

'Nothing great has ever been achieved without enthusiasm.' Ralph Waldo Emerson, Philosopher. (Quote from http://www.goodreads.com/quotes/14785-nothing-great-was-ever-achieved-without-enthusiasm)

If you enjoy yourself at an audition, so will the casting director. Casting directors can see thousands of people for one role;. make your audition one of their highlights.

The casting director is your friend. No one wants to work with a miserable person. Or a negative person. The casting director wants to give you the part, then they can stop looking. Always remember that the casting director is on your side.

Top Tips for Auditioning

Present yourself well. This includes your headshot, resume and covering letter. You are a whole package. Make sure that all of your marketing material had the same message and shows you in the best possible light.

Dress to suggest the character. If you are auditioning to play an office worker then wear a suit. Use your common sense.

Research before you go in. Research the story, the director, the casting director and the other actors. Try to watch the previous work of the director. Remove any obstacle that stops you getting the part - driving licence, accents, singing etc.

Look at the scene heading, is it an interior or exterior (INT or EXT) scene? Is it night or day? What page number is it? If you are on page three then you are at the beginning of the film and the characters are still being set up. If you are near the end of the script then most of the story has already been told and the film is now on the third act, the end.

Make decisions about the character but don't judge them. You cannot judge your character. You will not play them well or do justice to them. Read the script and take a note of the following things:

Who am I?

Who does the character think they are? Have a trigger name for their history. Think about their profession. Research your character so when you ask, 'Who am I?' you know the answer and it then triggers the life story of your character.

What are the circumstances?

What are the circumstances of the scene? Why is your character there?

What are the obstacles?

What is the obstacle of your character getting what they want? Know your character's obstacles and know the obstacles in the scene.

Where am I?

Where is the character? What time is it? Are you inside? Sitting down? Play the circumstances of the scene.

What does your character want?

It is very important to know what your character wants. In the scene keep playing the character's intent and the emotions as if your character is trying to get what they want. Everyone wants something. Find out what drives your character. Have an objective. It is better to make a choice and for it to be wrong than to make no choice at all. The director must see you acting. If they don't like it they can direct you to try it a different way.

Audition like a star - as if the part is already yours. Turn your nerves into enthusiasm and blow them all away.

Claim the casting; take the space and the time. Do not rush. This is your time to show what you can do. If you just want it to end that will come across. If you focus too much on what you want then you will not focus enough on the journey getting there.

Have a personality and push your personality through. Don't be too contrived. Everything should be natural.

Never let the camera lose your eyes (this doesn't mean stare into the camera, something you should never do!). Don't keep looking down at the script. If you cannot remember your lines then hold the script at eye level, away from your face.

Play an inspired choice. The casting director will have watched hundreds of actors play the scene you are doing. Make yourself stand out. Play high stakes and take a risk. People will remember you. Dazzle them.

The moment the casting director says the word *Action!* you should be in character. Stay in character until you hear *Cut!* or know that the scene is over.

Sight reading is important. Take a sight reading class if you feel you need to.

Be generous and easy to get along with. No one wants to work with a rude or difficult person. Keep whatever is happening in your private life out of the audition room.

How To Be A Successful Actor. Becoming an Actorpreneur.

The script tells you everything you need to know about the character and the story.

Make sure audition speeches, if you do more than one, are really contrasting. Give them something different. If they are not contrasting then you will just be showing them the same emotion. You will look like you do not have any range.

Begin acting the moment you meet the director.

Research all of the people involved, flatter but only genuinely. Don't be fake and make sure you get the accent right.

Be enthusiastic. Act like you want the part but do not be desperate.

Take the director's questions and comments into consideration, adjust accordingly. If constructive criticism is given then be thankful. Too many people react negatively to constructive criticism but it really does help you grow and improve.

Avoid speeches with props, or that involve another actor talking.

Don't think of it as a speech. It is a slice of your character's life.

Play the changes of thought in the script.

Watch your body language. Your whole body has to suggest the character, don't just read the lines. We only address someone by name for a reason. Use punctuation in the script as a guide. Know what to do with your arms. Amateur actors are usually easily spotted because they never seem to know what to do with their arms on stage. Don't overthink it.

Be flexible. Listen and respond to the director. Learn to take direction well.

Thoughts read in the eyes. Remember this.

Keep the acting in the eyes, not in the forehead

Your eyes are your main tool, learn to use them to tell your character's story. Acting is thinking, but thinking hard. Play your emotions in your eyes.

When you focus on the scene, the blinks come at the right time.

Watch out for dead face. This means you do nothing and are blank when the other actor is talking. When the scene is not focused on you, listen and react to the other actor. This sounds basic but you would be surprised how many actors don't do it.

Possess an inner monologue. Always be thinking and in the moment of the scene. This will make your character rich and watchable.

Do whatever works and don't get caught up in 'acting'. You don't have to put yourself through the

How To Be A Successful Actor. Becoming an Actorpreneur.

mill and it is not good for you to do so. If you have to cry, get a tear stick. Using tricks or faking it does not make you less of an actor. Filming is expensive and you have to do whatever you can to get to the required emotion.

Cover and continue if you make a mistake. Don't stop or apologise.

Don't change the script. The writer will probably kill you. (I'm kidding. Possibly)

It is just as important to memorise what is important in the scene as the lines.

Own the part. Act like it is already yours. Claim the role. Have confidence.

Warm up before you step through the door. Do not be embarrassed. Warm up before you go into the audition.

Play the scene as if you already have the role and are at the first rehearsal. This will make you less stressed.

The camera loves to see different things. Make sure there is contrast, discovery and change. Have you ever noticed when you watch television that when the characters are talking they are usually doing something else too? This is to make the scene more interesting and natural. We rarely, if ever, stop to do a monologue in real life.

'With any part you play, there is a certain amount of yourself in it. Otherwise it's just not acting. It's lying.' Johnny Depp (Quote from http://www.brainyquote.com/quotes/quotes/j/johnnydepp169428.html)

Always remember that you are a storyteller. So tell the story.

'You're only as good as the chances that you take'. Al Pacino. (In a magazine interview)

Be able to listen, this is very important as it is what acting really is. Listening and reacting. The camera loves a good listener

Always listen to the director's and the casting director's notes. If you respond well to the notes and can take constructive criticism then you will be closer to booking the role.

Listen to the other character in the scene and work well with the actor. Bounce off each other. It is an amazing experience to work with a talented actor. It also makes your job easier. A good actor will bring the emotion out of you and make you up your game. Be present with them in the scene. Ask them if they want to run through the scenes a few times before you audition if you think it will help.

Work on your on-camera technique. If you have done a lot of theatre it might be worth taking a class.

Your reaction to the other actor is as important as your line delivery. But do not overplay it.

How To Be A Successful Actor. Becoming an Actorpreneur.

Say goodbye to everyone, leave no one out. Shake their hand and thank them for seeing you. Send a thank you card to the casting director. Manners cost nothing.

If you really make a mess of an audition then don't beat yourself up about it. Everyone makes mistakes sometimes. Michael Fassbender said that when he went to Los Angeles that; 'I was auditioning for television roles but I made a terrible mess of most of them and was quite intimidated. I felt very embarrassed and eventually went back to London with my tail between my legs.' He then said that he was too desperate for the jobs and the constant rejection was killing his soul: 'I made a balls of so many auditions. Lost so many jobs.'

Fassbender also has this pearl of wisdom which you should always remember: 'Fear is a healthy thing - it keeps you disciplined. You have to make sure you've done your homework.' (Quotes from Hollywood Reporter via Frost Magazine: http://www.frostmagazine.com/2012/06/michael-fassbender-on-being-poor-and-oscars/)

How To Be A Successful Actor. Becoming an Actorpreneur.

Chapter 7: After You Have Booked The Job

Do not rest when you get a job: promote it heavily, send out an email update to your network, network with new people and use your free time to find your next job. Work begets work. If it is a big job then hire a publicist.

Film Studio Locations

Black Island Studios
9-11 Alliance Road, W3, 0RA.
Nearest Tube: Park Royal

BBC Television Centre
Wood Lane, Shepherd's Bush, W12 7RJ.
Nearest Tube: White City or Wood Lane. (I always go to Wood Lane)

Bray Studios
Down Place, Water Oakley, Windsor, Berkshire, SL4 5UG
Get train from Waterloo to Windsor or Paddington to Maidenhead. Then get a taxi.

Duke Island Studios
2 Dukes Road, Acton, W3 0SL
Nearest Tube: Park Royal.

Ealing Studios
Ealing Green, Ealing, W5 5EP
Nearest Tube: Ealing Broadway or South Ealing.

Elstree Film Studios
Shenley Road, Borehamwood, Hertfordshire, WD6 1JG
You get the train from Kings Cross or West Hampstead to Elstree and Borehamwood.

BBC Elstree Studios
Clarenden Road, Borehamwood, Hertfordshire, WD6 1JF
You get the train from Kings Cross or West Hampstead to Elstree and Borehamwood.

Greenford Studios
5-11 Taunton Road, Metropolitan Centre, Greenford, UB6 8UQ
Nearest Tube: Greenford.

Leavesden Studios
South Way, Leavesden, Watford, Herts, WD25 7LS
Take train from Euston to Watford Junction. Then take a taxi.

How To Be A Successful Actor. Becoming an Actorpreneur.

Longcross Studios
Chobham Lane, Chertsey, Surrey, KT16 0EE
Train from Waterloo to Longcross or Waterloo to Virginia Water. There is a gate at Longcross you will need a code for. Be aware of this.

Pinewood Studios
Pinewood Road, Iver Heath, Bucks, SL0 0NH.
Train from Paddington to Slough. Then take a taxi.
Tube: Uxbridge is the closest. Then take a taxi. It is possible to walk but not recommended as there is no proper path and some random driver will probably toot at you and say you have a nice butt.

Shepperton Studios
Studio Road, Shepperton, Middlesex, TW17 0QD.
Nearest Tube: Hatton Cross and then a 15 minute taxi ride.
Train from London Waterloo to Shepperton. Also goes from Kingston. Then 10 minute taxi ride.

Teddington Studios
Broom Road, Teddington, Middlesex, TW11 9NT
Take train from Waterloo to Hampton Wick. Short walk from station.

Three Mills Studio
Three Mills Lane, London, E3 3DU
Nearest Tube Bromley-by-Bow.

Twickenham Studios
The Barons, St Margarets, Twickenham, Middlesex, TW1 2AW
Train from Waterloo to St Margarets. Then a short walk.

Costume House Locations.
If you have to go for a costume fitting it will usually be at one of these three locations.

Angels
1 Garrick Road, London, NW9 6AA
Nearest Tube: Hendon Central Underground Station

Carlo Manzi
31-33 Liddell Road, NW6 2EW
Nearest Tube: West Hampstead.

Cosprops
469-475 Holloway Road, London, N7 6LE
Nearest Tube: Holloway or Archway.

There may be a better way to get to where you want to go so always check Transport for London's Journey Planner. http://journeyplanner.tfl.gov.uk/

How To Be A Successful Actor. Becoming an Actorpreneur.

Films: On Set

Congratulations! You booked the job. Now the hard work starts. Making a film is hard work. Early call times, 12-hour days, hot lights, dodgy weather...the list is endless. I have been working on a film and looked at my watch only to realise that in seven hours I had to be back on set. I was still in costume and lived two-and-a-half hours away...don't let anyone tell you acting is easy work.

A call time is when you are due to be at the studio.

Tell the 1st or 2nd AD (assistant director, literally the assistant to the director) if you leave the set or have to go to the loo. It will take a while to set up the cameras and lights so you will probably have time.

When filming master shots keep the editor's job in mind. Hold the emotion for a moment after the director says cut. Remember that even though you got the part you could always end up on the cutting room floor. This has happened to me more times than I can count, and it is a sad and hard fact of the acting world.

Days or weeks after you book the job you will be sent a call sheet. The call sheet will tell you your call time, what scenes are being filmed and will have the contact details of everyone who is working that day. If you are lucky and the budget has enough money you will be picked up in a car and driven to the location. If you get a really good job a car will be sent for you. You will then be shown your greenroom or trailer, and then you will have breakfast. You will go to makeup, hair and costume and then you will wait to film your scenes...and wait, and wait.

Seriously, bring a book. I have been known to read a book a day while filming. People play cards too. Filming is hurry up and wait. This is because the set ups (the lighting and camera position) take so long and because they may be filming your scene last. Films are not filmed in chronological order. You could be happy in the morning and filming a death scene a few hours later.

In your trailer, or the greenroom, make sure you have things to do. Knitting is popular, as are crossword puzzles and reading books. Get up and stretch your legs. You can go over your lines but you should already know them before you get on set.

The food on film sets is vast, usually delicious and free. Not really a good combination. Try not to go too crazy or the costume department (costume) will be giving you evil looks while trying to stitch your expanding girth into your outfit weeks later.

When you have done your scenes you will be wrapped. That means you get to go home.

A car will not always be sent. In fact you will usually have to find your own way to work. Make sure you are on time.

It is worth noting the emphasis on London. Although there is acting work all over the UK (and beyond), most work happens in London and a lot of the film studios are here or just outside. As are most of the auditions.

In the theatre

How To Be A Successful Actor. Becoming an Actorpreneur.

Doing theatre is an amazing experience. I will never forget performing at The Garrick in the West End. For films you may or may not be sent a car. For theatre you probably won't. Theatre usually has a few weeks' rehearsal period. Get to the theatre early to warm up before you go on stage. Few things are more exhilarating, and as scary, as doing theatre. With theatre there will be a rehearsal period. For two to four weeks you will rehearse and then it will be lights up. Less hurry up and wait, more go, go, go.

Chapter 8: Staying In Work

You would be surprised how many successful actors have to take other jobs to survive. *Hollyoaks'* and *Holby City* actor Jeremy Edwards now works as a labourer and says that he 'does not know any actors who work consistently without other work, but I had a good ten year run.' (Quote from http://www.dailymail.co.uk/tvshowbiz/article-2031605/Former-Holby-City-star-Jeremy-Edwards-says-hes-happy-graft-pay-bills.html)

Nikki Blonsky couldn't find other work after being in the film *Hairspray*. *Hairspray* made her famous but she had to find a job working in a hair salon, earned a cosmetology licence, and as of December 2011, was working as a hairstylist in her hometown of Great Neck, New York. Blonsky stated that she has not given up on her acting career.

Amy Adams said that she could not find a job for two years after starring opposite Leonardo DiCaprio in Steven Spielberg's film *Catch Me If You Can* and Michael Fassbender said that he didn't work for a year after he landed a part in Spielberg's television show, *Band of Brothers*, an experience Fassbender said, 'taught me to save my money'.

Salma Hayek told *Stylist* magazine in October 2012, 'I'm grateful to everyone who gave me an opportunity, but strangely there haven't been that many. I've had to fight very, very hard for every silly, small role.' She went on to say that when she first arrived in Hollywood at the age of 24 directors used to kick her out of the audition room after they heard her accent. She went on to make *Frida*, which took her eight years. She cast herself as Frida and says, 'the only part I had was the part I gave myself.' Salma says she still struggles because she is short, foreign and over 40. Depressing, right? But that is what you have to do: if people are not giving you the roles you want then start your own production company and cast yourself. Or even just make some films with your friends.

Angelina Jolie said early in her career: 'I am doing my best just to keep my clothes on and not be cast in girlfriend roles.' (Quote from http://www.interviewmagazine.com/film/new-again-angelina-jolie)

Scary, right? Just when you think you have made it another thing happens. This is why an acting career is not for sissies. In fact, one of the best things you could do for your acting career is have a flexible, well-paid job that can run alongside your acting career.

How To Be A Successful Actor. Becoming an Actorpreneur.

Captain Phillips actor Barkhad Abdi may have won a BAFTA and been nominated for an Oscar, but he was struggling financially during the awards season in early 2014. He was paid $65,000 for the film but had not booked another role. Acting is expensive so if you get one film and then don't work for a while then you have to survive on that money, you must learn to save.

The Independent said: "When production wrapped, Abdi returned to Minneapolis and a job at his brother's mobile phone shop. During the publicity campaign for the movie, Sony Pictures - which produced Captain Phillips - would put him up at the Beverly Hilton hotel. The studio also provided clothes and a car, though only for official publicity events. Recently, The New Yorker reported, "Abdi requested that he be allowed to stay at a commuter hotel near [the airport] to be closer to his friend, a Somali cabdriver from Minneapolis, who shuttles him around for free." (Source:http:// www.independent.co.uk/arts-entertainment/films/news/captain-phillips-actor-barkhad-abdi-struggles-despite-oscar-nomination-9171593.html)

Be patient and persistent. Keep taking classes.

When you do start getting work it is also your choice whether or not you only take certain parts. Do not let other people's opinions decide on what films you take, you never know when your next job will come. Read this pearl of wisdom from George Clooney, 'People go, why did you do *Return of the Killer Tomatoes*? Because I got the job, asshole!' (Quote from: http:// www.huffingtonpost.com/2012/01/23/stars-diss-hollywood-clooney-edgerton_n_1223315.html)

I have turned down certain parts but usually because of nudity or other reasons.

Top Tips to Stay in Work.

Make yourself as wide ranging as possible. Be able to sing, dance and act. Learn martial arts and take a stage combat course. Learn how to shoot a gun and learn a new language.

Learn to promote yourself. People have to know you exist to hire you. People can also forget you. So keep in contact with people you have worked with.

Motivation

Successful actors are highly motivated. You cannot be a successful actor and be lazy. People do not have 'accidental' film careers. It is hard and you really have to put yourself out there, again and again after constant rejection and criticism. When you read an interview with a Hollywood star and they say that they fell into acting and were just in the right place at the right time they are lying. I am not kidding. A successful acting career is not a happy accident. It is a lot of time and hard work.

You have to go to the gym and stay in shape. If you cannot afford the gym, or just do not want to get locked into a contract then work out at home. I love Zumba and the Tracey Anderson Method. Keep training, apply for castings every day.

Email people promptly, update your website and resume on casting sites. Learn accents and skills. Socialise and get yourself out there. Sorry if this seems repetitive but you have to constantly put the work in.

How To Be A Successful Actor. Becoming an Actorpreneur.

Being an actor is a business and you are the product. You may not like to think of it that way but if you do not look after yourself then how can you expect other people to hire you? Acting is the most competitive industry in the world. It is not for the meek.

If it all gets too much then take a day off. Go for a walk and get some fresh air. Just spend a day relaxing and having fun. Whatever it takes to recharge your batteries.

Networking

Networking is incredibly important. If people don't know you exist then they cannot give you a job.

As your career progresses, the majority of the work you get will probably come from one or two sources. Get yourself out there but not in a cynical way. Network to meet like-minded people and make friends. If you are hating every minute and are just using people for their contacts or for what they can do for you it will just backfire. Don't be transactional. Be friendly and sociable. Be generous with your knowledge and contacts. Always have business cards on you. You will never know when you will need them.

Shooting People do a first Monday networking event. Raindance also do a networking event. If you are female join Women in Film and Television. They do a lot of networking events that a number of people have told me are excellent.

See And Be Seen

It is true that being seen in the right places can help your career. The acting industry is oversubscribed with an ever-dwindling job market, so reminding people that you exist could get you an all-important job. Some of the places to be seen are The Phoenix Club on Charing Cross Road. The Bar at the National Theatre, Soho House, the Groucho Club, Blacks and the theatres around London, Glasgow, Edinburgh, Manchester or wherever you live.

If you do not live in London there will be places to network. Go online and do some research or ask some other actors.

Having The Edge

Marilyn Monroe once said, 'I used to think as I looked at the Hollywood night, "There must be thousands of girls sitting alone like me, dreaming of becoming a movie star". But I'm not going to worry about them. I'm dreaming the hardest.' That is what you have to do. You have to dream and work the hardest. You have to want it more than anyone else. You have to work harder and train harder. You have to be better than the competition. (Quote from http://news.bbc.co.uk/dna/ place-lancashire/plain/A26655555)

You have to stay in shape and apply for castings, keep up your classes in dance, singing and acting, do workshops, market yourself. Acting is more than a full time job, and despite the fact it takes so much work you will not be paid for any of this. In fact, you rarely get paid to audition but it does happen. I got paid £50 to audition for *Goal 3*. Which I was very pleased about as I had to travel all the way to Nottingham.

How To Be A Successful Actor. Becoming an Actorpreneur.

Equity

The main union for actors is Equity. Costs start at £9 per month and go up the more money you earn. To get your Equity card you need to have trained for three years at an accredited drama school or have professional credits. It used to be hard to get an Equity card but now it is relatively easy. You just need to have trained or have some credits. I am a member of Equity and they have helped me out a number of times.

Equity have a magazine that they send out to members, as well as a diary every year. They also do events, give advice, provide insurance and you can also get discounts with your Equity card. Go to http://www.Equity.org.uk or more information.

Chapter 9: Hints and Tips To Further Your Career.

Business Cards

Get some business cards. You can get good cheap ones from Vistaprint or Moo.com. Get a good design and have your name, mobile number, occupation and website/Spotlight link on too.

You could (and should) also get business cards which have your picture on. These are very good as people will remember your face and hopefully cast you from them!

Go to Shooting People and Raindance networking nights. Hand out business cards with your name and contact details on. Tell them that you would love to come to any screenings that they have.

It is important that you follow up with the people that you meet. Just drop them a quick email that it was nice to meet them, mention where you met and ask them to stay in touch.

Pitfalls.

Another depressing thing about this industry is that if you come from a family with no money you may find it hard to sustain a career. Downton Abbey actor Rob James-Collier said this to the Radio Times in 2012:

'You have to work for a year with no money. How on earth are you going to finance that?' he asked and said he had found it hard to make it as a 'working class lad.

The acting industry is full of Oxbridge graduates and people who went to public school (private school for American readers). These include Thandie Newton, Alexander Armstrong, David Mitchell, Olivia Williams, Sophie Winkleman, Eddie Redmayne, Tom Hardy, Dominic West, Henry Cavill, Freddie Fox, Benedict Cumberbatch, Sophie Okonedo, Colin Firth, Helen Bonham-Carter, James Purefoy, Tom Hiddleston and Damien Lewis to name a few.

James-Collier, was raised in Stockport and he told the *Radio Times* that the acting industry favours the wealthy. He worked in manual labour jobs to fund his acting dream.

How To Be A Successful Actor. Becoming an Actorpreneur.

'Because you've done the horrible jobs it gives you an even grittier determination to succeed,' he said. 'If I had a comfort blanket, I wouldn't have been as passionate and driven. When you get there, you really do appreciate it because you know where you have been.'

He also said that his mother had been supportive and that his father had allowed him to try his luck.

Another tip is to use flashcards for your character. Films are usually not shot in sequence so have a flashcard for each scene which will easily let you know what your character is feeling at that moment and what emotions are required. They really do come in handy.

The differences between the mediums should be learned. Theatre is bigger, you play to the

crowd and you project your voice. Film and television are similar but you will probably have more dialogue on television and have more scenes to film each day. Film acting is subtle. It is thinking, but thinking hard. You should play the emotion in your eyes.

Know who you have worked with. Keep records and business cards. This will prove invaluable when you try and get your next job.

Make sure that you audition well on tape. Buy a camcorder and record yourself. Find out what your flaws are and correct any bad habits. Buy a microphone and learn how to do self-taped auditions. (see auditions chapter)

You just have to keep working. The more you work, the more other people will hire you. Success reaps success.

Fourwall magazine is a good magazine for actors. It also has a website with a lot of advice. http://www.fourthwallmagazine.co.uk/

Have notepads full of ideas but be careful - go through them, take notes and throw some out. If you just have notepads full of ideas then that is what they are: ideas. You have to put your ideas into practice.

I love the story that Michael Fassbender told the Hollywood Reporter in 2012: [first acting role of note was in HBO's *Band of Brothers*, which aired in 2001. He was confident it would lead to other offers. It didn't.] 'I came to Los Angeles and did auditions for television. I made a terrible mess of most of them and I was quite intimidated,' he recalls. 'I felt very embarrassed and went back to London. I got British television jobs intermittently between the ages of 23 and 27, but it was very patchy.' Between roles including a Guinness commercial (in which his character swims from Ireland to New York) and a one-off, *Agatha Christie's Poirot*, he took odd jobs to survive, unloading trucks or bartending. He even did market research. 'I had to call people who had filed complaints about the Royal Mail and see if they were happy with how their grievances were dealt with. Most of the time they weren't'. All along, he says, 'My goal was for acting to become my main income. I would say to myself, "I'm good enough." That became my mantra.'

It is not essential to get an agent. You can get work without one. Though maybe not access to some of the top jobs. If you can't get an agent and cannot seem to be able to catch a break then write your own scripts and make some short films. After you have made them, enter them into festivals. It is a good way to get seen.

You could even get a job in the film industry for a while and try and make contacts. Befriend as many other people as you can. It is important to build a good network around yourself. Write your own material and get it made with you in the lead role. Network as much as possible. Do a weekend directing course and make your own films. Get a new agent if you are not getting any auditions or you feel you have outgrown each other.

Develop a vision of your own career. Take more classes and learn new skills.

I met American casting director Daryl Eisenberg and the advice she gave for actors was: "You are not special". Do not think that you are special and are going to just make it. You are just like everyone else. Daryl also said that it is important to remove whatever is not getting you hired.

Chapter 10: Public Relations and Marketing

Be your own PR person and generate hype around yourself. When *The Herald* listed me as one of the Top 50 Young Scottish Film and TV Stars under 30 it had an immediate impact on my career. People became more interested in me as I had mainstream publicity behind me. I then emailed casting directors telling them this good news and I got positive replies. This was something that had not really happened before. A casting director will probably read the email you send them, but they are so busy they rarely reply. I never take this personally. They are just busy people. One of the casting directors I emailed was reading a script at the exact moment I sent them an email and called me in for an audition for one of the parts. Proving that this business has a large element of luck involved.

Make sure you always have some Black and White, and colour 10 X 8 portrait head shots as well as some 5 X 7 ones and even some in postcard size. Have a reserve for signed photo requests (you will be surprised at how quickly that can happen, even a little role in something can make someone ask for an autograph) and casting directors.

IMDB, Who Represents, Cast, SAG, Ata's Agent Search, Breakdown Service, LA Casting, Academy Player's Directory, and Google search are all useful. Use them to locate people as well as to find jobs.

When you are in a production of note contact all free listings, local papers and local radio. Write to the arts editor of your local paper, *Time Out* and *The Stage*.

Postcards are amazing marketing tools. They are basically just postcards with your headshot and your contact details. Union status, representation, website address, highlight of credits and a wonderful photo. Use them next time you do a mail out.

Have a website that uniquely markets you and keep it updated.

Use mailing lists and viral marketing to get your message out.

Be google-able. Google yourself and make sure there is good stuff out there. People have to be able to find you.

Keep everything updated. I know I have said this a million times but it is important.

Interact with any fans who write on your message board on IMDB or the comments board on your website or blog and ask for autographs. If they leave nice comments you can also thank them.

With photos, people look at the first three and the last one.

How To Be A Successful Actor. Becoming an Actorpreneur.

Have a Twitter account, a Facebook page and a blog. And, as ever, keep them updated.

Also check out a site called Karmalicity. (http://www.karmalicity.com) It lets you get likes for your Facebook and IMDB page in return for liking someone else's page.

Websites

Keep it simple. Update regularly. Avoid flash as it takes too long to load and might not work for some browsers. It has to be able to load quickly and without fuss. Have your resume, showreel, pictures and contact details on.

Have a page for each section: Resume, biography, contact, showreel, gallery, press and reviews and voice-over.

Include some good links to other sites as this will make the google rank of your website improve, making you rank higher in the search engine. Ask friends to link to your site or link exchange with other sites.

Include links to your IMDB, Spotlight and other sites on your website.

If you have a blog also put the link to it on your website. Same goes with your Twitter and Facebook fan page.

Try and make sure that your website coveys what you have to offer. Make sure it reflects some of your personality. Also make sure that the focus is on your acting. If you do other things leave them off the website. You do not want the message to get muddled or for people to think that acting is just a hobby.

Use important keywords towards the top of the page. Google cannot index a photo but it uses key words and text to index your website. Link words to other relevant websites as google will weigh them up more.

Submit your website to Google, Yahoo, YouTube and other search engines.

Don't muddle your image. Know who you are and know your market.

Use Search Engine Optimisation. SEO will make sure that your website comes at the top of Google's search engine. Hire an SEO company to make sure you are the first actor to come up when people search for your type.

What you have chosen is a very hard career. 95% of actors are out of work at any one time. If this 95% did not have another job they would be well below the poverty line.

Castings happen quickly and mostly on the internet. So make sure you maintain an active online presence.

Social Media

How To Be A Successful Actor. Becoming an Actorpreneur.

Social media is a great thing for actors. So many things have made life easier for actors in recent years. Facebook and Twitter are two of those. You can build a following on Twitter and Facebook, follow casting directors, other actors and directors and even look for castings. Be on Twitter and Facebook, and also have a Facebook page. Keep it updated but work-focused. Be careful what you tweet, you have no idea who will read it and you cannot delete it permanently. Even if you remove it, it can still come up in search engines.

Link your Twitter to your IMDB page. A word of warning though, if you delete a tweet it is still on your IMDB page and they are kept in chronological order dating back years. Be careful what you tweet! To remove your tweets just remove your Twitter account from your IMDB page. If you put it back again later, the tweets will still be deleted.

Keep your political opinions to yourself and don't tweet about your hangovers. Keep away from anything negative and offensive. People in the entertainment industry hire people who can play nicely with others. If they don't think you are going to get along with other people on set, then they will not cast you.

Media Attention and PR

As you become well known you will start to attract attention from the general public and also the media. I get asked for my autograph on a regular basis and I am only a working actor. If someone asks for your autograph via your email or website try and get your agent to deal with it. You do not want to give your contact details out to people. Although most people do genuinely want an autograph there is always a small chance that the person may be a con artist or someone unstable.

If someone wants to interview you, say yes! There is rarely such a thing as bad publicity. But never bad mouth someone in public. If you come across as negative or mouthy in the interview it may stop people hiring you. You are your own brand. Have high standards at all times.

A note on IMDB and the Star meter.

IMDB is a great resource, not only does it have a page on every movie and every film industry professional you can think of, it is also an amazing tool for an actor to promote their career.

IMDB has a resume section that you can join for a reasonable price. When you have IMDB Resume you can add pictures to your IMDB, and of course your resume. You can also link your blog and your Twitter to your page.

When people Google you, it is usually your IMDB link that comes up first, so it is a false economy not to have it. If you do not have a project on IMDB (and you need one! Work for free for an IMDB credit is my advice) then you can still be on it if you get IMDB Resume.

People do lie on their resume, but I don't recommend this, and do not list extra work unless you were heavily featured or had a line.

Even more important than IMDB Resume is the IMDB Starmeter. This is IMDB explaining what the Starmeter is http://www.imdb.com/help/show_leaf?prowhatisstarmeter

The Starmeter is important for actors and here is why: if you get a good Starmeter ranking that

How To Be A Successful Actor. Becoming an Actorpreneur.

means you are bankable. It goes from 1 and then into the millions. 1 is the best so a lower ranking is good rather than a higher one. If people are searching for you then you will be offered movies and auditions. My Starmeter has been as low as 6,000 and is usually between that and 31,000 on a bad week. Which is very good news and has helped my career. So, if your IMDB rank is not very good what can you do? I previously wrote about this in my personal blog http://balavage.wordpress.com/2011/07/25/charting-imdb-becoming-obsessed-with-starmeter/ and I am going to go into more detail here.

Step 1) This site is very good. http://www.karmalicity.com/b/?r=218 I know people who have done barely anything who now have good rankings, the site gives you publicity for your IMDB, Facebook fan page, YouTube and Twitter. It is free so join now. The premium version is cheap and very good too.

Step 2) Make sure you have your photo on IMDB. It is very important. Also put film stills and on-set photos on and modelling shots as well. If you want a photo, you can click the following link and go to add photos only: http://resume.imdb.com/

Step 3) Use social networking. Post your IMDB link. Add it to your email signature, your website, Twitter, anywhere you can think of. Share the films you are in, not just your IMDB page, every time a movie you're in goes up, so do you.

Step 5). Create an e-mail list. Only email when you have something to say or people will get sick of you. Do not spam people. Invite people to a screening, tell them of an award you won, an amazing job you just booked. Add your IMDB link into the email and email signature.

Step 6) Get people to click on your IMDB profile (post the link on your Facebook or Twitter profiles, have it in your email signature, etc.)

Step 7) Get interviewed and mentioned in TV guides and news articles.

Make it a goal to get in the Top 5000.

To round up; IMDB is an amazing resource to help your career and I wish I had paid more attention to it earlier. Click on your friends' links and put nice comments on their message boards and ask them to do the same for you.

Chapter 11: Acting Abroad

The acting industry is very much alive and kicking in the United States of America. Primarily in Los Angeles and New York. If you want to be an actor the best places to live are Los Angeles, New York or London.

Los Angeles is the one that comes out on top. More castings happen there in a week than in the rest of the world combined. Los Angeles is the centre of the film industry and every actor should go there at least once in their life. If you are serious about having a film career you will probably end up there. However, the advice that I have had is to wait until you have been invited. There are hundreds of thousands of actors in Los Angeles so you should try and build up a career in the United Kingdom (or wherever you live) first. You will also not be able to work without a visa. You will need a Greencard or an 0-1 visa. (read Alison Winter's interview in the interview section for more information on how to get a visa. You will also need a lawyer and it will cost an estimated £2000 if you include legal fees). You will also need to be able to drive as no one walks in Los Angeles and it is very spread out. You can use your UK licence for a year and then you will have to get an American one. You will also have to perfect your American accent. Otherwise you should just stay home.

(Tip: You cannot travel to America without a return ticket unless you have a visa. So always buy a return)

Pilot season in Los Angeles is between January and April. Pilot season is when all of the big networks commission new ideas for television shows, which then have to be cast and made. If you are going to go, go then and try and land a show. If you land one it will pay amazingly well. Even $28,000 a week according to one friend. Even if you are not a big star.

New York is more theatre and television based. Of course there is Broadway, their version of the West End, and a lot of good television shows are filmed there, and films too. In New York you can walk everywhere and will not need to drive. New York and Los Angeles are on opposite sides of America. So choose which one you want initially. If you really want to be a film actor, head for Los Angeles.

Americans take acting classes very seriously. They are big on continuous training. If you train with a specific acting coach then it can really add to your resume.

After you get a visa you will need a social security number. And remember that there is no National Health Service in America so you will need health insurance.

My main advice on moving to America is not to do so unless you can work there legally. If you do not have a visa you will not get a job. Casting directors always check. In fact, you will not be able to even get a normal job and you could also be deported, fined $10,000 and banned from America. So get a permit!

How To Be A Successful Actor. Becoming an Actorpreneur.

New York's Spotlight is called the Players Guide

The Los Angeles version of Spotlight is the Academy Player's Directory.

To work in America you need an 0-1Visa or a Greencard, a good American lawyer, time and money. A manager on the US side will also help and you will need to have an American agent. You're American accent must also be flawless and you will not be hired if you do not have a visa or a green card. Another recent development is that some studios only hire actors with a Greencard, an 0-1 visa is not enough. This changes from studio to studio, but a Greencard is best.

Casting is global now. It is a globalised market. You do not necessarily need to move to Los Angeles or other places. It is enough to live in a city, especially as self-taped auditions become more popular.

Perfect a few different accents. American, English RP and any other nationality that you look like. If you look Italian, then perfect your Italian accent.

Keep your national identity though. It is your Unique Selling Point. Use it.

Chapter 12: Top Tips.

On camera do not wear hats, stripes, white, loud patterns, loud colours, be careful with jewellery and perfume.

Wear neutral solid coloured clothes that are tight fitting.

If you find your mouth dries up with nerves, scrap your tongue hard against the back of your teeth.

Always remember that your character has already lived through this. Remember their past.

Dress to suggest the character. But do not overdo it.

Keep an audition diary and keep a record of what you wore and looked like in each audition. Note who you audition for and who else was in the room. Write down any important information that is worth remembering.

Learn about contracts, billing and how much you should be paid. Contact your union if you are unsure or cannot find the information online.

Make the subtext important.

Character is craft plus attention to detail.

Acting is a powerful metaphor for living

A good actor does not act: a good actor creates.

In tennis you learn the strokes then forget them. In acting you learn your lines then you forget you learned them.

It is important to account for lapses in jobs and training. Make your life sound full and exciting even if you have just been watching television.

Think like a casting director.

An actor has to be trained to be in the world of illusion. You have to sell this imaginary world to the audience. People will give up reality for illusion.

Humans are the only creatures who dilute themselves. Remember people wear a mask. Your character may have a motive, but they should try to hide what they want from the other characters.

Humanity is the secret to all acting.

How To Be A Successful Actor. Becoming an Actorpreneur.

Acting is the only art you cannot be caught doing.

Remember that we like to watch people try and save themselves.

Sight reading (when you do not know your lines and just read from the page as you go) is not a good look. Try and learn your lines. Be off book. Don't make excuses.

Prepare as much as possible.

'An actor's job is to show up knowing his lines' Anthony Hopkins.

Make up looks depend on the audition, but at least even out your skin tone. If they ask you not to wear make-up then don't. It will just make you look insecure and vain.

Know as much as possible. Google people and research what else they have done. Watch their previous work to get a general tone and learn their style.

Look just off the camera. Focal point near the lens. Do not look directly at the camera. It's unprofessional and breaks the fourth wall.

Martin Scorsese talks about the psychic power of the lens, and he is right. The camera can pick up your every emotion. Do not use this as an excuse though. You must still act.

Do your best to learn the lines, if not, remember the essence of the scene.

Relax.

Never mention a negative work experience in an audition. You do not want people thinking you are difficult to work with or that you talk behind people's backs.

Replicate the first audition in the call back.

Research everyone, what they have worked on and what they look like. Knowledge is power.

Compliment people. Know what they have worked on and show respect.

Don't over prepare or judge the character. You don't want to learn the lines so well that you just say them in parrot fashion. Also memorise the emotion behind the scenes. Don't just say your lines. Think the scene through. Always be aware of your surroundings.

Know where you should be standing and make sure you are lit properly you should step into the light where it feels hottest.

Have a playable action for the scene.

How To Be A Successful Actor. Becoming an Actorpreneur.

More importantly: enjoy yourself and work hard. Be sociable and friendly when on set or at the theatre.

Chapter 13: Finding the Next Job

This is most important: an actor's career is made up of jobs from various individual directors but as the career develops, most actors find that their work comes from, over and over again, the same relatively small group of people with whom they have worked on numerous occasions.

One of the reasons acting is such a hard industry is that you put so much work into getting a job, then it ends and you need to get another one. You really should be trying to get your next job while you have one. This may not be possible as most working days in the film industry are usually 12 hour days. But keep abreast of what is happening, contact people, apply for castings and keep your agent updated.

Use the fact you are working to try and get some publicity. You could hire a publicist if you get a job that is high profile enough. The more people know you and your work the more you will be hired for jobs.

Use Facebook and Twitter to let everyone know you are working. Update your website and update the 'currently appearing in' section on your Spotlight page.

If things dry up then make some films of your own or start a theatre company.

Because it is harder for females, if you are female then join forces with the males who have made it. Never be afraid to ask for advice. Ask people to meet up for some tea or coffee. Most people I have met in the industry are very giving and generous.

If you do a commercial keep track of when and where the advert appears to make sure you are not owed more money than the buyout you were paid.

Write to casting directors; make sure your cover letter is concise. Research casting directors and know who casts your type. When watching television and films take note of who cast the project. Keep records.

Know your type. Know yourself. As you grow older your type will change through the years. This is not a bad thing and don't get obsessed with ageing. The older you get the less competition there is. Acting has a high dropout rate.

Identify your type, create one central image for your marketing campaign. Set yourself apart from the competition. Make sure your headshot stands out in thumbnail size. A lot of the time this is all someone on a casting site will see when they are searching for actors. Have active eyes, targeted to your market.

If Things Get Quiet

How To Be A Successful Actor. Becoming an Actorpreneur.

Don't worry if things go quiet. Even the best actors can go for a year without getting any work.

If you are not getting any auditions or work then remove whatever it is that is not getting you employed, get your driving licence, learn to dance, sing, take some new classes.

Get new head shots and update your showreel. Email people who you have previously worked with.

Make more contacts. Go to the film festivals that are near you. If you go to the Raindance Film Festival you will meet a lot of directors and the British Film Institute does the London Film Festival which is also worth going to.

If you are female join Women in Film and Television (WFTV). They do preview screenings and networking events.

Make some films. I love this story about how Stel Pavlou, director of *The 51st State*, made his film: 'I made sure that [the film] wouldn't cost too much and that it was all larger than life, characters coming out with mad dialogue. Lark Aldridge (producer/friend) and I realised a trip to Cannes would get thing moving. But red tape meant we needed an official stamp on our application. I told him to find potatoes. He asked me what the hell I was talking about. I told him to get a knife; cut a big letter 'F' for our logo on the potatoes drop in some ink and stamp the form. He did it, sent it off, and within days we had producer badges. We spent a week in Cannes, hooked up with Focus Films who put up the development money and from there we haven't looked back.'

You need business skills, persistence and patience to make it as an actor. It is not a sprint, it is a marathon.

Send your headshot out to casting directors, producers, directors and production companies. Include your resume and a covering letter along with a stamped addressed envelope.

Do good work. Even if you have to produce your own theatre shows.

As you get older your type will change. Determine what market niche you are best suited for.

Watch some television and films and find out what casting directors cast your type. Make a list and send all of your details to the casting director. Either via email or by post.

Reconsider head shots, update resumes, get a voice tape and showreel in order, get picture cards, a website, create a database of producers and directors. Connect with your agent and get together.

Evaluate your strengths and weaknesses and then work on your weaknesses. Take classes, study, and get on top of your marketing.

Do whatever you can to meet new people. Join professional directors' organisations, acting classes and casting directors' workshops. You just need one person to give you a job, then another.

Do not make the classic mistakes of just being interested in acting and film. You have to take an interest in the world and be able to play a human being. Study history, politics, finance, art and read the newspapers.

If you really want to be an actor you really have to put the work in. It is not for the work-shy. Be as proactive as you can. Make sure you keep in contact with your network and know if there is any projects being casting.

It is also a fact that some actors will always be more successful later in life. It can also take years to build up momentum. Michael Fassbender (him again, sorry, but every actor can learn a lot from his struggle to make it) struggled for over a decade to become successful and had this to say about his struggle: 'I trusted myself from the start and I just believed. I kept knocking at the door and at some point there was a crack and I got my toe in. Once I got my toe in, I got the rest of my foot in and the next thing, I was in the room.' (Quote from http://www.irishexaminer.com/lifestyle/features/a-hunger-for-the-big-screen-155863.html)

"It doesn't pay to get discouraged. Keeping busy and making optimism a way of life can restore your faith in yourself" - **Lucille Ball (Quote from** http://www.goodreads.com/quotes/ 18459-it-doesn-t-pay-to-get-discouraged-keeping-busy-and-making**)**

There are also exhibitions where you can go to meet people in the industry and other actors. They are:

Actors Expo

The UK's first, biggest and only dedicated trade show and exhibition for actors and performers. The next one is in Camden, London. I have been a few times and it is worth going to. I also end up meeting lots of people that I know. A lot of industry people go. (http://actorexpo.co.uk/)

Surviving Actors.

Surviving Actors was set up by actors for actors to help and encourage them in all areas of their life as a professional actor. The convention falls into three sections - Develop, Sustain and Create.

Events run throughout the year and introduce actors to the various ways of making money outside the profession, using their craft to their advantage, ideas to develop their career; and different opportunities to create work.

Surviving Actors is free to attend and is worth going to. It usually has good talks and seminars. You can gather good information. It is also good for meeting like-minded people. (http:// www.survivingactors.com/)

Chapter 14: Your Marketing Tools.

To be an actor you will need a resume, showreel and a headshot. These are your marketing tools, and getting them right can make the difference between booking roles and never getting seen. Take the time and the effort to get these marketing tools right. Always try and put yourself in the position of the person receiving your CV/showreel. You want to be professional, you want to stand out and be memorable and you don't want to be boring or put your audience to sleep.

CV/Resume

Your curriculum vitae is important. Keep it on one page and put your best work first. Put your name in bold and add height, contact details, agents contact detail, hair colour, eye colour, union affiliations, Spotlight pin, website URL, credits, skills and playing age.

For your credits, separate them into Film, Theatre and Television. Put your best credits first and drop the older, less impressive ones as your career progresses.

It should go without saying but you must have a specific resume for your acting. Don't put any non-acting stuff on your resume. Don't just print off your Spotlight page. Although you can do that, it looks better if you don't. You can find an acting resume template online for free. Just google 'free CV templates'. Some computers and laptops also come with free writing software that includes resume templates.

Spin your resume. List your best work and add all of the skills you have. Name the title of the project in the first column and list the most impressive thing about it.

Use all of your brand names. List anyone famous you have worked with or anywhere famous you have worked. People respond to brand names and it will make your resume more impressive.

A resume is not just a list of things you have done. Itemise your projects honestly but in a way that best showcases you.

Remember that brevity is the soul of wit: get to the point. Have your name and the name of your credits in bold. Have nothing over one page in your resume or letter.

Cover Letter

A good covering letter can get you an audition. Make the casting director laugh or smile and you may be half way to booking a job. Keep a template that you can tweak for specific jobs. Try to show some personality in your cover letter. Casting directors get hundreds of applications for every casting so if you make them laugh or stick out in some way it really helps. I have done castings so I know this. For email covering letters include your Spotlight pin, IMDB page link and your website. Even just in the email signature.

How To Be A Successful Actor. Becoming an Actorpreneur.

Reference something in the breakdown from the casting and say why you would like to audition for the role.

Have your IMDB page, website, etc. at the bottom of your email signature. The more hits you get to your IMDB page the higher your Starmeter ranking. The higher your Starmeter ranking the more noticeable you will be in the industry.

Always find a contact to send your covering letter to. Never write Sir/Madam. Try to avoid the obvious. No, 'I am an actor' or 'My name is...', that will be obvious. Try to stand out and not be boring or predictable.

Try to use good paper. Good stationery is much more important than people think and can help your covering letter stand out. It seems obvious but do not write it by hand unless you have the most amazing handwriting in the world. Type it out and then sign it.

Paragraph one should be an opening statement, which encapsulates you in two or three short sentences.

Paragraph two should be a note on what you are currently doing or have recently done.

Paragraph three should be a brief summary of your availability or some interesting facts about you. You should make sure your covering letter is interesting and that it will stand out from hundreds, and possibly thousands, of other covering letters. Sign off with a good and appropriate greeting and also include your contact details. Your headshot, CV and covering letter can get separated from each other so staple them together and make sure you have your contact details on all of them.

After you have finished your covering letter read it over and make sure that it puts your personality across. Also make sure it is easy to read. Ask some friends to look over it and give their opinion. Check for spelling and grammar mistakes.

Letter writing

Or email writing to make it more accurate these days. Though some casting directors do not have their email address in the public domain. To write to a casting director, either write to them about a specific role and tell them about why you could play the role, if you are updating them on something you have done or keeping them updated then keep it concise and to the point. Casting directors are busy people so the less time you take of theirs the more they will like you. Just tell them what you have done, a little bit about yourself and include some links to your website or Spotlight.

You can get casting directors' email addresses and office addresses from Contacts, The Actor's Yearbook or from IMDBpro.

Personalising each letter

Address your letter to an actual person: it is unlikely to get read otherwise. If you have met the casting director before then mention it. If they previously cast you in something mention it and

66

thank them. If you have seen a film they cast that you like then mention it.

Showreel

Your showreel is important to your career. In fact, it is probably more important than your resume. I have been hired after people have seen my showreel. Acting is a visual medium, you are more likely to be hired when people can see what you can do.

The best thing you could do is have a memorable scene in your showreel that people will remember or find funny. My showreel has a memorable scene that includes a threesome gone wrong. I have had quite a few jobs from people loving that scene and thinking it is funny. Check it out at http://www.catherinebalavage.com

Never have a showreel that is over three minutes long, and even that is too much. Also have a one minute demo speed reel. Don't do montages and make sure the action focuses on you and not on the other actor. Make sure you are speaking in all of your scenes in your showreel. If you don't have enough footage just use what you have, but make sure it is good and shows that you can act.

Do a one minute speed reel and another that is two and a half minutes long. It should be all of your best work. You can edit your own showreel on your computer. It is very easy to do. Showreels do not have to be perfect. They just have to show you off to the best of your ability.

Make sure your showreel has good sound quality and includes your contact information.

Make sure it is not too long and boring. It must showcase you. Have your name at the start of the reel along with your contact details.

Don't have too much of the same material. It will look like you have not done a lot of work. Better to do a shorter showreel with stronger, different material than one that makes you look like a beginner. A flashlight only works on the strength of its weakest battery.

The showreel should show you off for the roles you want to play. Try and include scenes with different accents. American and RP are good ones.

The showreel should show variety and depth. Try doing different accents and playing different parts and try and show some range.

Put it everywhere, on YouTube and your website. Make sure you put the link in your email signature, along with your IMDB link.

Your showreel tape could be composed of television or film appearances. Local programmes, student films or independent films are all okay. Don't include filmed theatre.

Chapter 15: Further Tips to Sustain a Career.

Register on all of the major quality casting sites and databases. Keep your name out there.

Things To Remember.

The business isn't fair. You can be the most talented person in the world and not 'make it'. Fairness does not come into it.

Physical discrimination is a normal part of casting. Whatever your physical attributes, they will contribute to how you are cast. You will not be cast for who you are, but how you look. I was told by one casting director that any dress size above a size 10 for women is considered a character actor. Your accent and looks will all play a part in the roles you do and do not get.

Let go of your vanity. You are an actor, not a model. You cannot act well if you are constantly thinking of your best angle. Everyone is vain to an extent but put the character first.

You don't have to be super thin, but if you are overweight you will be cast differently. As long as you are confident, you will still be able to book work.

Talent doesn't always rise to the top. Don't think just because you are talented that you will make it. Talent is not enough. You need stamina, passion and persistence to have a successful acting career.

Scene Analysis

Study the text and know the character. Look at the given circumstances. Look at where the scenes is set, what time it is and what is happening.

Play the action, focus on the specific actions and play them with an economy of movement. Do not overact on camera. It doesn't work. Film acting is subtle.

Pace is always a consideration in comedy, be quick, comedy is rarely slow. In comedy timing is everything.

Look at the page number to know where in the film you are.

Fringe Theatre

The fringe theatre scene is buzzing in London. There are a lot of very talented people doing fringe theatre for no money or profit share. It is a great way to keep your instrument sharp and casting directors do go to try and spot unknown talent.

How To Be A Successful Actor. Becoming an Actorpreneur.

Unfortunately there isn't any money in it. Most are profit share, and there is usually no profit. It is still something to consider and try to get on the resume. The Edinburgh Fringe and the Edinburgh Festival are also great ways to get out there and be seen. As well as being a good experience.

Making Your Own Films.

In many ways it is not enough just to be an actor now. Lots of actors are now writing, producing and directing their own work. If you are not happy with the roles you are being offered or you are not getting much work then you should start doing your own projects. You can make a short film with some friends or take it more seriously and try to get it into film festivals. Brit Marling did this with Another Earth and then she ended up on the cover of Vanity Fair.

You can also start up your own theatre company or comedy group. You could also do a web series to keep your name out there. I did one with some friends and when I later went to castings people had heard of it.

If there is no money, do it for no money.

Headshots

I know I have said this before but it is important enough to say again: make sure your headshot looks like you. Don't wear too much makeup (this includes men) and make sure your hair is not too different. Wear a neutral colour but not white because the photographer might use a white background.

Wear a V neck top, a shirt or a scoop neck. Do not show a lot of cleavage unless it is appropriate for the roles you are going for! Look professional. Do one smiling and one not smiling. A variety would be good and get it photoshopped but just for spots and dark circles, nothing else. Do not have your hands in shoot. Do not show too many teeth and make sure you are not too stylised. Make sure your eyes are showing some emotion and do not have any props in the picture. The headshot should just be about you and your type.

Headshots in Britain are usually in black and white but colour is becoming more popular. In America headshots are always in colour. Keep your headshot updated every year. It is expensive but essential.

Make sure you have your correct contact details everywhere.

Make sure you have your current hair style in the headshot. If you change your hair, you need new headshots. I once did a commercial and one actor had been hired to play Madonna on the strength of her headshot, which was a picture of her with short, blonde, curly hair. Very Madonna in the 1990s. When the actor turned up she had long red hair. The director was very upset and told her that she should have gotten a new headshot. Filming had to be stopped and a new Madonna had to be found. You do not want to be this person. I have never seen this actor on set again. Word gets around.

Try to suggest a type with your headshot. If you do not know what type you are then ask your agent or friends and family for their opinion. Try and think about the type of role you usually get cast in. It is important to know the type of roles that you can play. You can always break out of typecasting after you start to get work.

Reproductions

After you get your headshot you should get some reproductions made. There are plenty of photorepro companies that will do this for you. Some are more reasonably priced than others. Search on the internet, ask friends for recommendations or get a copy of *Contacts.*

A note on postage

Make sure you have the correct postage. You will win no fans if the casting director has to pay to receive your resume and headshot. This actually happened to me when I first started acting and the casting director was actually really nice about it. Do not try this approach though. It is not worth the risk.

Casting Directors

The most important thing to remember about casting directors is that they are human. You don't have to be scared of them and see them as people who are trying to stop you from getting a job. They want you to be good. They want you to get the part. If a casting director brings you in for an audition they are taking a risk on you. If they bring you in for an audition they already think you are good. All you have to do is show them your version of the character and prove them right.

Most of the casting directors I have met are wonderful, creative people. Just look at them as a fellow industry professional. Don't be too friendly however. Sycophancy won't get you anywhere.

Don't be scared of casting directors. They are on your side. Try and build a friendship with casting directors. Don't bombard them with emails or calls. Make sure that you don't spam them! Be professional at all times.

Casting directors also do workshops. They usually cost about £30. These may be worth doing just to meet casting directors.

When a casting director helps your career send them a thank you card or some flowers. Show gratitude. Manners are underrated. Also keep casting directors who have brought you in or hired you updated on your career.

Nudity

Only do nudity if you are comfortable with it. Just because you are an actor does not mean you have to take your clothes off. If you do have to appear nude, ask for a modesty patch. This covers your, ahem, bits.

Unfortunately, a lot of female castings come along with 'nudity may be required'. If you are not comfortable with nudity, then don't do it. If you are comfortable with it, ask for a closed set. Unfortunately females are asked to get naked much more than men. While women are widely expected to take their clothes off, for men it is such a rare event that when Michael Fassbender did full frontal nudity in *Shame* it was widely commented on and he experienced quite a lot of good-natured ribbing during the award season.

Interviews

In interviews be friendly and professional. Always have something to say and show some personality. Don't try and second guess people, just be honest, intelligent and witty. Don't make yourself sound like a struggling actor who needs the job. Make your life sound interesting. Do not be desperate.

How to Dress

Dress to suggest the character. If you are doing an audition for a police officer then wear black trousers and a white shirt. If you have piled on some pounds then invest in some Spanx. They are really big in the film industry and thin you by half a dress size approximately.

Don't forget your hair. If you are auditioning for a period film then wear your hair a special way. If your character is a bit of a free spirit don't go in wearing a bun.

Chapter 16: Other Avenues of Work

There are many different avenues for work in the acting industry. TIE (theatre in education), theatre, commercials, video games, TV, film, role-play, voice-overs, corporate videos, demonstrating, teaching, pantomimes, music videos, narration, singing, dancing, presenting, hosting, If you expand your horizons you are more likely to earn a living.

Voice-over

Voice-over work is lucrative but hard to break into. Get a professional voice reel done and shop it around. Try and get a voice-over agent. Look at *Contacts* and send it off to some agents. Email people who you think may hire you with a link to your voice reel.

If you want to get started in radio presenting try starting at a local radio stations and work your way up. Write to the BBC Radio Drama Department and ask to join the list for general auditions.

With voice reels don't be versatile, people don't hire versatile. Do your own accent. Do not do too much. Put it all in a padded envelope. You can use some different accents after you get your foot in the door and only if you are really good at it. Avoid page turning as the microphone will pick this up.

Phone an agent with the right approach. Use your voice to sell your voice. Research agents and find one that does not have your voice type on their books. Then send them your voice reel and resume and let them know that they do not have a voice actor of your type.

Day Jobs

Having a flexible day job can be vital to make your acting career work. As I mentioned earlier desperation can negatively affect your auditions and mental state. The key for a successful job is flexibility. You might need to suddenly film for six months and you'll need a job which can accommodate this.

There are a number of ways to make money when resting: Promo work, temp work, mystery shopping, merchandising work, painting and decorating. You need a flexible day job that you can drop at a moment's notice. If you are interested in Promo work join Stuck for Staff. http:www.stuckforstaff.co.uk. It costs £25 per year.

All of the jobs above will be on acting sites. You can join agencies like Gekko and Channel Advantage if you would like to earn some good money demonstrating products. Join as many temp agencies as possible.

Acting is full of administration. You must keep all of your receipts and also keep a record of auditions and who you met and when. The more organised you are, the easier your acting life will be.

Always be contactable. You can easily miss out on a job. Have your phone on all the time and always check emails and messages.

Always confirm auditions and jobs by text, email or by a phone call.

Chapter 17: Tax and Health

Tax.

You have to register with HMRC three months after becoming self-employed or you could be fined. Hire an accountant if it all gets too much and remember to keep all of your receipts. Keep a record of your income and outgoings too. Bookkeeping is essential. The good news is that a lot of your outgoings will be tax deductible.

Keep all of your receipts. You will need them for the end of the tax year. Don't lose them or you can't claim the items as tax deductible. You need to keep your receipts and everything to do with your tax for six years.

The following things are tax deductible for actors:

Travel

Any travel related to acting work is tax deductible. This includes auditions, rehearsals, fittings and the work itself.

If you use a car, motorbike or bike there are two methods for claiming. The first method is to claim a fixed mileage rate. Check the latest rates with HMRC. The second is to record all your fuel costs and claim a percentage based on the mileage related to your acting career. Parking fees for acting related work are also deductible. A percentage of MOT, insurance, car security is also tax deductible. Speak to an accountant or HMRC if uncertain.

Clothing

You can only claim for clothing which is part of a performance or premiere. You can't claim for clothes to auditions unfortunately. They need to be 'wholly and exclusively' for your business.

Agent Fees

Fees charged by your agent are tax deductible. This will include the amount plus any VAT they charge. Booking fees are also tax deductible.

Accountant

Hiring an accountant is tax deductible.

Equity, Casting Sites and IMDB

Equity, casting sites and IMDB are all tax deductible.

Telephone Bills

A mobile or landline used solely for acting is tax deductible. If a phone is used partly for acting an estimated percentage of both the line rental and the phone are tax deductible. I would advise contacting your accountant or HMRC if unsure about this.

Make up

Any makeup or hairdressing bought for work is tax deductible.

Hotel Expenses and Food

As an actor you might often find yourself needing to stay in hotels when filming or auditioning. These costs are tax deductible. Be aware though that it is more complicated if your family are staying with you or you extend your stay beyond when you are working. You should seek advice on what to do in these cases.

If you are staying away from home on location, you can claim for food and drink as long as it is not an excessive amount.

Computer Hardware and Software

A percentage of your computer hardware is deductible if you use it for research and looking up castings. The same is true of iPads and tablets. You can also claim a percentage off software you use for your work and for printers and USB drives

Other Tax Deductibles for Actors

Film Magazines
Dental Work
Marketing Expenditure (Creating a showreel or voiceover, headshots)
Gym Membership
Stationery and Postage
Cinema tickets, DVDs, books and theatre tickets (for research)
Web Domain and Hosting Fees
Networking Events
Acting Classes (although not all drama schools take advice on this)
Singing Lessons

Health

You have to stay as healthy and as fit as possible when you are an actor. Your body is your business. The working days are also long and you will need lots of stamina. You will also have to stay in shape. The camera does not add 10 pounds, it adds a lot more!

Exercise, drink water, take a multivitamin, eat fruit and vegetables and get enough sleep.

How To Be A Successful Actor. Becoming an Actorpreneur.

Consider joining a gym (which is tax deductible) or if you can't afford it try and find an alternative you can do in your house such as Zumba or an exercise DVD.

Teeth

Look after your teeth. This is especially important if you go and work in America. They don't make jokes about 'British teeth' for nothing. Teeth are incredibly important and will stop you get getting certain parts if they are not right. Dental work is tax deductible for actors. You should consider getting braces if you need them and you are serious about your acting career. You should use a whitening tooth paste and should consider getting your teeth professionally whitened if you can afford it. It's also important to floss. Do not go too far in the other direction, having teeth which are too white might be a bad thing. If they look unrealistic it could stop you getting a part.

Read a lot

You should read as much as possible. Read plays, books, newspapers and magazines. Be well-read and it will show. Know what is happening in the world. This will also help you with your networking.

Observe people, know about them. You have to know about humanity and how people work. Their thoughts and what makes them do what they do are your business.

Give yourself an advantage by learning skills other actors don't have.

Being able to fence and ride a horse (not at the same time) will vastly improve your career. These two skills are usually in demand. Martial arts are a much-used skill in the film industry. Having martial arts training will open up a whole new genre of films and potential work. Learning about firearms and how to use a gun is another useful skill. Knowing another language can also give you an edge over the competition.

Costume

When you are in costume it is your responsibility not to ruin it. Try to not drop food over it or tear it. It won't win you any fans in the costume department. Look after your costume.

Wearing a corset: breathe out when they are putting it on. Don't let them make you laugh or breathe in. This is a trick costume people use, don't fall for it! Eat little when you are wearing a corset as you will expand and the corset won't!

Join the Actor's centre. You will meet like-minded people and there will be a range of classes there that will further your career.

Chapter 18: The Interviews

I have been lucky enough to get access to, and interview, some of the main people in the acting industry. I have had good advice from the people at Spotlight, Casting Call Pro and StarNow. I have also interviewed some top casting directors, actors and agents. I have included some interviews from other people in the industry to give you a feel of it. I feel I have been given some really good answers and that after reading these interviews you will be more enlightened. Read and learn.

Simon Dale from Casting Call Pro.

Simon is one of the founders of Casting Call Pro. Casting Call Pro is one of the main casting sites for actors.

What was the idea behind the business?

We'd worked together in online recruitment for the film and TV industry for four years, working at The Production Base, a service for all those behind the camera (e.g. editors, camera operators, sound recordists, runners etc.), so we knew the industry. Chris's sister was graduating from Mountview and was paying substantial subscriptions to a number of casting breakdown services. We realised that with our background and technical expertise this was an arena we could enter.

How did you make it a success?

Crucially, we wanted to offer members more than a simple directory listing. With this in mind we built community elements in addition to the casting breakdowns - we wanted to bring the actors tools to help develop their career. Hence the directories of agencies, photographers, theatres, schools... and the community aspect to the site. Individuals, schools and companies are now using it to track and stay in touch with friends, alumni and old colleagues. We also offered a very different model to the other services out there in that we offer a completely free profile listing in the directory - which has helped us grow to our current size of 25,000+ members. We do have a premium subscription, but the profile listing is entirely free.

What mistakes do actors make?

Some have an inflated sense of their 'right to perform', perhaps down to ego, perhaps thinking that the mere fact of undergoing training entitles them to a lifetime of work. The harsh reality is that it's a very competitive field whose daily currency is rejection. It's hard to be seen for parts, harder still to be cast - that's simple mathematics, there will always be a huge number of people up for the same part, many of whom will be talented. And so often (especially for commercials) it's less about

How To Be A Successful Actor. Becoming an Actorpreneur.

the depth of the acting talent and more about the surface look.

We hear about actors who breeze into an audition having done no preparation, no background research, not even having learned the lines they've been given. Sure, there will always be stories about people who stroll in, shoot from the hip and land the role. But you're taking a huge risk if that's your general modus operandi.

What advice can you give to actors?

Be proactive - don't expect work to come to you. Try and find an agent if you don't already have one. Network with people, attend industry events. Go to as many auditions as you can - it will help your technique and even if you're not cast you are still in front of the casting directors. I have a friend who was up for a part two years ago - she didn't get it, but the casting director contacted her eighteen months later with a role she thought she'd be perfect for. Difficult as it is, try and remain positive. Rejection day in day out is, inevitably, going to wear you down at some stage. Remember that you've chosen to enter an incredibly difficult profession, and that you might not be landing the roles may not be down to your acting talent. Keep the faith!

What advice can you give to other people starting a similar business?

Plan ahead. And plan ahead some more. Prepare your budget, make realistic forecasts. Bed yourself down for some lean times at the outset. We left well paid jobs to set up Casting Call Pro. We took huge risks and made personal sacrifices. We worked without salary and had to put in an awful lot of time and effort, not knowing if, further down the line, we would have a successful service (though of course we believed that we would, or we wouldn't have taken the risks!). Look at the business holistically. As you grow, operating a business becomes so much more than running the core service that you set out with. You'll need to learn about finances, PAYE, VAT, Corporation Tax... you'll be interviewing and employing staff, running an office - all the while trying to run and expand your original business idea. For small companies (less than twenty employees) it probably won't be feasible or necessary for you to hire HR staff or in-house accountants and lawyers - so you'll be wearing many hats, office manager, bookkeeper, HR....

It's likely that at some point in the first two years you will hit a low - financially or emotionally. You're putting in all the work but not seeing the returns. These are absolutely pivotal times - most businesses fold within the first two years. If you retain your belief then you might turn the corner. We had to get different jobs to pay the bills, but we didn't give up. And then we turned the corner and have never looked back.

What it the best thing an actor can do for their career?

Find an agent. Be proactive in trying to independently find and put themselves up for auditions (though do keep your agent informed). Train. See as much theatre, film and television as possible. Periodically reassess their career and drive - and, if necessary, give themselves a metaphoric shot in the arm to keep their spirits up. (Remember all the positives, your ambition, your passion - those things that first inspired you to get into acting).

What is the funniest casting you have ever had?

Among the strangest we've had are requests for actors to play pranks on bosses and ex-partners, as well as an over-zealous salesman who was offering an all-expenses-paid trip to Helsinki for anyone who was willing to impersonate his CEO at a client meeting the real CEO couldn't attend.

What do you think of actors paying for casting director workshops?

It's entirely up to the individual. Sessions with CDs seem to be on the increase. Research the company providing them, and the CD(s) themselves. What have they cast? These seminars and workshops can vary enormously - some being straightforward talks, panel discussions, Q&A, and even interactive sessions at which the actors perform a piece and receive feedback from the CDs. As with all these things (casting services included), ask friends and peers - what do others think of them?

What is next for Casting Call Pro?

As ever, we'll keep developing the service, building new features and adding new tools to try and help the actor and to better our service. Already we have expanded out from actors to create allied sites for dancers, stage crew, film crew etc. Watch this space!

Casting Call Pro is an excellent website for actors. To find out more and to join follow the link http://www.uk.castingcallpro.com/

Lyn Burgess.

Lyn Burgess is the no.1 personal and business coach in the entertainment industry. Go to http:// www.magickey.co.uk/ to find out more.

I came across Lyn Burgess and her coaching a few years ago through Creative Edge Audio, a range of CDs for actors which had advice from people in the industry in audio form. I was very happy when she said yes to being interviewed. I find Lyn incredibly inspirational. I hope you do as well.

How did you get into personal and business coaching?

I worked for many years in operational roles in the financial services sector and was made redundant from an HR Director's job. I had outplacement consulting and looked at my skills and my values and out of that came 'coaching'. I think I always had a coaching philosophy though when I was managing teams of people, I always found I could get them to do what was needed without wielding a big stick - and they'd be quite happy to do it as well. Setting up my own coaching business in 2002 seemed like such an obvious progression, I'm not sure why I hadn't done it before!

Best tip for confidence?

'Fake it till you make it!' It's good to model someone else who is a confident person - give yourself a 'confident outfit' or a lucky pair of knickers. Start off by just 'pretending' to be confident for 30 minutes each day and experience how it feels. Make sure you have some interaction with other people and see how differently they react to you. Also, create a visualisation of you being/feeling confident. Practice this every day. Also think back to a time when you felt confident so you remember that you can do it and notice what happens in your body. Start little and often and your mind will become the confident person you want to be

What do you love about your job?

Pretty much all of it. You won't ever meet a coach that doesn't enjoy what they do - they always want to do more, help more people. I love marketing my business, I love networking, I love finding new places to advertise, I love working out how to reach more people, how else I can coach them. I love other people's success and knowing that because I helped them set some goals and asked them a bunch of questions it really made a difference to their lives and their career. I also love doing presentation and workshops to groups of people. You get some great energy back and participants always learn from other people.

Advice for actors?

Be tenacious, get clearly focused on exactly what you want i.e. a part in a period drama at the Globe starting in October 2010 paying me £X, rather than 'I want a job'. The latter kind of statement is useless; if that's your idea of a goal then go work in Tesco - there, you have a job. Never give up, and be proactive. Having an agent doesn't mean you can sit at home and wait for the phone to ring. You can switch on the TV and see that being an actor is not necessarily about being talented. You need to be in the right place at the right time, knowing the right people and not having any hang-ups, or moaning about the industry and telling yourself how tough it is. Network your butt off. It's much easier to make connections face to face, rather than sitting in a pile of CV's. Make it easy for casting directors and agents - put yourself in a box to start off with. Once you get well known, then you can diversify, but if you look like a thug and sound like a thug, play thugs.

Who is your inspiration?

Three people. One: An old boss of mine who saw potential in me and would always say 'Lyn, I want you to go and do such and such a job now,' and I'd think, 'I'm not sure I can do that' - then I went and found that I could do it. Every two years he gave me a different job role to do and it just made me realise that you can do things that you are unsure about. He believed in me and that enabled me to believe in myself. Two: Fiona Harrold - A UK life coach. When I first started my accreditation to become a coach I read her book *Be your own Life Coach* and I felt so inspired I knew I was on the right path. Three: Tony Robbins - a US life coach. He does the fire walk which I have done - which is actually really easy to do. Check him out on YouTube or read his books, he's awesome.

Tell me about your workshops?

The workshops I run on a monthly basis and they cover 3 main themes. They were born out of doing some advertising when I first started out on Shooting People where I wanted to get into the minds of people in the industry and offered some free coaching in return for completion of a short questionnaire. I had about 90 responses and realised that was a lot of free coaching! So I set up the workshops so that I could coach a whole bunch of people at the same time, rather than one to one. The workshop topics are : Focus, we work around goal setting, looking at what holds you back and create an action plan. Self-Belief - on this one we look at limiting beliefs from your past, blast them out of the way and look at confidence building. Networking: where to go, what to say, how to follow up etc. etc.

What is your background?

Financial Services - and by that I mean processing mortgages and secured loans. I also worked in two Building Societies. I started as a secretary and then held managerial roles for years. I have done acting and theatre directing, so I know what it's like to stand on a stage - which I loved. I always found that I could relate to most people (even if I didn't like them) so it was always a career that involved interacting with others. Financial services was great because it was fast moving and you had to constantly change and be flexible and I think life is like that too. Every few years you have to reinvent yourself because the landscape keeps changing. I love that, I love taking risks. Too many people try to be a perfectionist and there's no such thing as perfection, you are striving for something you will never attain. Do something, get a result, tweak it and then do it again!

What's next?

I feel like this question should be at the end. One of the things that I've always wanted to do is to work more with people on a project and within a team of people i.e. on a TV programme or on a film. So work with the writers, the producers, the directors and the actors and be part of the production team for whoever needs me. Help with issues of time management, working to budgets, stress management, team dynamics etc. I want people to say in years to come 'God, we never make a film/TV programme without a life coach!' It always helps to have someone disassociated from the project to look at it in an impartial way to give those in it another perspective. I also have an idea for a book called *Life, Camera, Action* which uses well known Film quotes to illustrate coaching themes - but I need a writer to write it - then I can develop it into a workshop to take around cinemas in the UK.

How To Be A Successful Actor. Becoming an Actorpreneur.

What does your average day consist of?

Variety! Coaching clients which can be via email or telephone. I don't do much face to face work apart from the workshops. Marketing, Twittering, advertising and promoting. Pulling together some ideas for joint workshops. Following up on contacts that I've met networking, or recently at Cannes. I never seem to have time to blog frequently enough. But I do promote an 8 Week Makeover Programme that is a very cost effective way of coaching. I also run the events committee for Women in Film and TV, so that usually forms part of my day, checking in with the event producers or organising an event of my own. I email the WFTV office several times a day.

What is the hardest part of the job?

Wanting to do everything right now and being impatient. I want to help more people, answer emails, Twitter, write newsletters, do my accounts. The hardest part when you first start out is getting to know the difference between empathy and sympathy with a client. I'm good at it now and have developed quite a good sense of emotional detachment. Coaching is always forward focused so it's my job to keep people 'in action' - the hardest part for me is understanding that people move at their own pace - not mine. I sometimes come away from a call thinking 'was I any use there? That person is not doing enough' and then two hours later I'll get a text or an email from the client saying 'thanks so much for the sessions, they are always really useful! So it's all about perception, and as one of my Magic Quips said: 'it might look like I'm doing nothing, but at a cellular level I'm really quite busy'.

For more on Lyn go here: http://www.magickey.co.uk/

Jessica Manins From starnow.com

I met Jessica after she hired me to do a talk on acting at an exhibition in South London. Jessica is lovely and professional. She really knows what she is talking about.

How many breakdowns does StarNow get a week?

Approximately 2000 new breakdowns globally ranging from acting roles to crew, model, dance and music positions. StarNow is unique in that it offers roles for all people in all areas of the industry and being a global website you can find work in Germany, France, UK, Ireland, South Africa, USA, Canada, Australia and New Zealand.

How did you get into casting?

I started acting from a very young age then moved into production. When my friends created StarNow it seemed the perfect place for me to work. Not only could I help other actors but I was able to work with casting directors, understand their role and what they were looking for.

The best bit about working in casting is seeing all the unique talent that comes through the site.

How To Be A Successful Actor. Becoming an Actorpreneur.

When a casting director asks me to help them it's often because they are looking for someone with a unique skill or look. Someone that stands out from the crowd. Thankfully we have 2 million members so it's never too hard to find them who they're looking for!

What is the best thing an actor can do for their career?

Find a skill that gives you a clear point of difference from other actors and work so hard at perfecting that skill that you become an expert. If you are the best at something then you create yourself a niche. Be it stunt training, weapons, languages, diving or horse riding. If you have something more to offer than just being a brilliant actor you become invaluable.

How does an actor 'make it'?

Hard work and perseverance. It also depends what your definition of 'make it' is. I know a lot of actors who have great careers, they work the majority of the year on projects they love. To me I consider they have 'made it': they have made acting their career.

Are they making lots of money? Probably not lots, but enough to live happily. Are they famous? No. But I don't think they care because they are doing what they love and they don't have the paparazzi following their every move! I believe if you are serious about being an actor then 'making it' is about being successful. Everyone has a different definition of what success is and it most certainly doesn't mean being famous.

How do actors sabotage their careers?

By not being professional. Like any career you need to be professional or you won't progress. I see so many actors sabotaging their careers by being unprofessional. Be it as simple as having bad headshots, turning up late to auditions, being rude on set to crew, not learning lines. There are all sorts of ways an actor can sabotage their career but all lead back to being unprofessional.

Advice for actors

3) Be professional!
4) Find a point of difference and work really hard on perfecting it.
5) Accept rejection and use it as fuel to carry on and work even harder.
6) Network like crazy.
7) Use social media to create a community and interact with others working in the industry.
8) Take classes/workshops that will help you develop more skills as an actor.
9) Make your own work.
10) Ensure you have the tools you need i.e. headshots, showreel, online profile, a phone, and an agent..

What is the most important thing an actor can do for their career?

Practice every day.

How many actors are on StarNow?

We have a database of over 2 million members globally.

How To Be A Successful Actor. Becoming an Actorpreneur.

What trends have you noticed in casting?

More and more castings are happening online and the traditional casting processes are disappearing. Actors are now able to submit themselves for roles and through the use of online technology they can do this from anywhere in the world. What was once a closed door industry that only the elite few had the privilege of being a part of is now much more open. There is the opportunity for unsigned actors to be seen by great Casting Directors as sites like StarNow offer casting directors new faces.

Should an actor ever do extra work?

This is a question that comes up a lot and different people will say different things. In my opinion when you're starting out in the industry extra work is one of the best things you can do. Look at it as a learning experience. It's a great way to understand how a set works, what the different crew roles are and give you a true understanding of how long a day in film actually is. If you think the film and TV industry is glamour a couple of days on set as an extra will quickly squash those thoughts.

Extra work can be a great way to earn some cash and give you time to practice your acting. There are generally hours of spare time in which you could write, practice your lines, listen to audio language or accent classes. Plus you get the bonus of meeting others working in the industry and as I mentioned earlier networking is a key element in finding success.

If you have an agent they may not want you working as an extra because they are marketing you as an actor. In the end I believe it's all about the individual. If you find being an extra is a great way to earn some cash while networking and upskilling as an actor then by all means do it. If you feel it will muddy the waters and directors might not take you seriously as an actor, then don't do it. Remember you don't need to put the extra work you have done on your CV.

Emma Dyson From Spotlight Interview.

Emma Dyson works for the main casting website for actors in the United Kingdom, Spotlight. She also does one-on-one talks for Spotlight members to give them career advice.

So tell us about you.

I'll tell you a bit about my background. I trained as an actor at the Guildford School of Acting in the 1990s and then, having got the training out of my system, I quickly realised I couldn't be an actor. I probably didn't have the talent or the perseverance or the backbone. Then I was an agent for six years. Then I left being an agent thinking that I would go into a different career, something entirely different, but every job that I was getting was pulling me back to the business so first of all I was working at my old drama school back at Guildford, I was the personal assistant for Peter Barlow who was the then assistant director, and then I left two weeks into the job because he was leaving. Subsequently a casting director put me in touch with Thea from United Agents, and I was temping at United Agents sort of off and on for about six months which is when I got the job here at Spotlight being the PR manager.

How To Be A Successful Actor. Becoming an Actorpreneur.

I used to do castings within the agencies and get the Spotlight breakdown and put roles and the actors that fit them together. It was interesting, having worked in an agency, because the first point of contact that you do in casting work is Spotlight. Now I am very happy here as PR manager and I go to the drama schools and talk about acting and Spotlight member benefits. How to get a good CV and photo, what type of letters to write to casting directors, agents. Time and time again they are incredibly green. They are in their final year of drama school and have hardly written any letters to agents or casting directors. They leave thinking 'Here I am, come and get me!' it just doesn't work out like that. It's really important and I empathise that it is very important to write letters, to hopefully reach your future employer, who will, across the course of your career, become your friends, and keep re-employing you.

It is such a shock when people leave drama school. They don't really know what to do.

I know and it is such a shame. They go to Central, LAMDA and RADA. Those are very central London schools. They get so spoilt for choice because it's awash with agents and casting directors, it carries the kudos of being at the best drama school. Where I was at Guildford we were terribly cut-off despite the facts it's only a twenty minute train journey, but, we *felt* very cut-off. It's a shame that schools that are not in central London get kind of left out and not thought of. There are some interesting actors in regional schools. The Welsh college is a very good school with a lot of good courses and a brilliant reputation. Conversely Rose Bruford has some really good students and that is in Kent.

I think you have got to train, you have got to workshops, you have got to keep classes going. Try to teach yourself as many skills and techniques as possible because the more skilled you are as an actor the more you should work. I always like the actors who go into musical theatre, straight theatre, film and do a bit of everything, And what we are noticing is that there is more of a vogue for musical theatre and films are being made from those musicals. I know of a few film directors who are making films which are musicals. It is kind of a renaissance or a nod to the 1950s. The MGM sort of musicals. Musicals are very popular.

So learn to sing

Learn to sing if you can, and if you can dance then I think you will probably work all the time.

Daryl Eisenberg, an American casting director, told me two things when I met her: One, you are not special. Don't think you are more special than anyone else and are just going to make it, and two, whatever is stopping you from getting a job, remove it. So if you can't dance then learn to dance, etc.

I think that is just a roundabout response to what I just said. If you do just keep yourself as skilled and as tuned in as possible then you will get work. You have to do as much theatre as you can and as much film as you can. Not only that but I extend it to: if you are a London actor or a London based actor see as much art as you can, culturally exploit everything which is on your doorstep. Because I think that tunes you in to everything. It keeps you aware of what is current. You pick up on working trends and that reflects across the arts.

Tell me about Spotlight events,

How To Be A Successful Actor. Becoming an Actorpreneur.

Yeah, we do events. Being PR manager. ..We did one in October in conjunction with the London Film Festival. I got three casting directors. I got Karen Lindsay Stewart and Lucinda Syson. It was held at the British Film Institute and it was chaired by Pippa, my boss, and myself, it was just about how to become a working actor, keeping your CV up to date, how to get an audition, and also I do seminars where I talk a lot about being a working actor, how to network, all of those things, and at Spotlight offices on every Monday we have Spotlight Mondays where I operate 20 minutes chats with people who are stuck in their careers. They are incredibly popular. They always sell out very, very quickly. And the seminars are sometimes in conjunction with Actors Expo or other bodies. We just hold little seminars in house.

How do you break through?

I think it depends because some actors burn out very quickly, and other actors, they see an opportunity and they become very successful and popular when they are in their forties. So I think it just depends because there is so much reliance on good luck and you have to have a lot of charisma, a lot of talent. But then the rest of it is luck. I think you can make your own luck, but a lot of it is out of your control. Probably one of the reasons that I didn't become an actor was because I couldn't stand being in a career with no control.

To answer your question, I think it depends on many things. They have to have a good agent behind them and the rest of it I think is luck.

What is the most common mistakes actors make?

Not being proactive, not writing letters to casting directors. Even with a good agent you should still do your own work. Not looking after themselves, not working out, not eating well, not networking, I think all of these things, the actor has to do that. It is part of their homework.

How many actors are on Spotlight

Just over 40,000

Wow.

There are a lot of actors out there.

How does that break down male/female ratio

Not sure what the percentage is. I guess there will be more women than men and there are fewer jobs for women.

How many in London?

I don't know the answer to that.

[Note: The most quoted number I get for actors working in London is between 20-27,000]

Describe your average day.

86

How To Be A Successful Actor. Becoming an Actorpreneur.

I don't have one. I have been doing this job for six months. My job involves going up and down the country, talking to drama schools. Spotlight have a Spotlight Showcase every July.

Actors can apply themselves now. How is that going?

I think it is going well. Agents don't really like it, but they have a setting where either actors cannot suggest themselves and leave it to the agents or the actors can nudge the intention of the agent so I think it has proved to be very successful. Our two main bread and butter punters, our customers if you like, are the casting director and the actors. So it seems good sense to empower the actor to suggest themselves for work.

How many people apply to join Spotlight every year?

Oh, loads and loads. We have a system that if they have not trained at an CDNT Drama school or an equivalent then they have to have four professional credits. Featured work, no commercial work or still work. We reject hundreds of people every year.

I went to drama school because back in the day having an Equity card meant you could work. Obviously now Equity is not so important, shall we say, the union isn't so strong. If you go to an accredited drama school then you are going to go straight though to Spotlight anyway. If they go to an accredited drama school they get half price of the full price and the following year they are half price again. It's not until the following year when they go into the adult directory that they pay full price.

How does an actor know what section to go into?

They should. It is quite worrying if they do not. If the actor really doesn't know what type of part they should be playing...then they are quite frankly....[laughs] They should ask their agent or their drama school. They should work that one out for themselves. The guide for the casting directory is more for the casting directors.

I always say you should typecast yourself then break out.

Yes, I think that is very important. Work out what your strengths are and play to your strengths. Know about your casting ability you have as an actor and just go for it.

What mistakes do actors make in auditions?

Not learning the words, not being off book, turning up late. Turning up inappropriately dressed. Being arrogant, smelling of booze. Lots of these happen and lots of these shouldn't happen. You have to treat it like you are your own business. You have got to turn up on time. You have got to be off book. You have got to be courteous and polite. I think with all of that on board. You might find that you give a cracking audition and you should nail the job and be a successful actor

I think it is just a lot of luck and a lot of hard work. Lots of people mistake acting to be a glamorous world and I think it is nothing but blood and sweat.

And maintaining positive friendships with these people. It's very important.

Martha Shephard

I interviewed Martha from casting site To Be Seen. To Be Seen is newer than Spotlight, but is worth paying for if you can. Martha gave some really good answers that you can learn from.

How many breakdowns does To Be Seen get a week?

To Be Seen receives approximately over 100+ job postings per week. This number is steadily increasing as the company grows.

Tell us about To Be Seen.

To Be Seen is an online casting and audition service for the entertainment industry.

The company was originally founded by an actor/presenter who wanted another way to get seen in the industry in addition to the traditional route of signing up with an agent. This led to the creation of an online agency, where all talent could represent themselves and get work.

Since then, To Be Seen has grown steadily in the UK and recently auditions have come in for other European countries.

Jobs are posted daily seeking actors, extras, presenters, voice-over artists, comedians, singers/musicians, dancers, models and reality TV contributors.

All levels and types of productions have been advertised on the website including student productions, low budget short films, fully paid feature films, TV productions, corporate videos, online series, theatre productions, comedy shows and reality TV series.

Talent can create an online profile detailing their experience, uploading photos and a showreels. To Be Seen members then apply directly for jobs advertised using their online profiles.

What is the best thing an actor can do for their career?
How does an actor 'make it'?
Advice for actors
What is the most important thing an actor can do for their career?

Perseverance:

Perseverance is key, this industry is very competitive.

Showcase your talent.

How To Be A Successful Actor. Becoming an Actorpreneur.

Your headshot photos can be the first impression that casting directors have of you so make sure they depict you well. You should be facing the camera and have a non-distracting background. Avoid wearing patterns or prints, keep your clothing simple in solid colours. Don't go crazy with the makeup, casting professionals want to see you! Adopt a relaxed friendly pose.

Having a good showreel is the difference between getting that audition or not. A professionally made showreel is absolutely essential. Your showreel should be approximately 3-4 minutes in length. Show your versatility by having a mixture of your acting clips. If you don't yet have acting clips to add to it then consider a monologue piece. Update your showreel regularly and always ensure your contact details are on it.

Network:

Attend relevant networking and workshop/seminar events in the acting industry, there are loads of them out there. You will meet people and companies that will give you advice and also you can swap tips with other people in the industry.

Remember it's free to create a basic profile on To Be Seen and you can use it as your unique webpage to show your details, acting credits, photos and showreel. You can forward your To Be Seen profile link to relevant people & companies in the industry, print it on your business cards & display it in your email signature.

Your Online Presence:

Google your name! Check your online presence and any searches you come up in.

Take time to complete your To Be Seen profile and always make sure it is up to date with your latest showreel and acting credits.

Ensure your Twitter and other social networks represent you well. Use your headshot photo in your profiles and display your To Be Seen profile link in your bio's.

Applying For Auditions:

You should only apply for roles that you are suitable for and have the skills for as per the casting description. Casting directors do not like sifting through applications of people who are not suited for the role!

The Audition:

Double-check the location of audition the day before and arrive 10 minutes early. Print out your CV and attach your headshot photo securely to it. Find out all you can about the company and director. Research the role and the character. Lines should be learned off by heart. Be the character you are playing. Dress to fit that character. Don't pester the company for feedback after your audition - check your mobile and emails regularly and wait for them to contact you.

Continue applying for further auditions - perseverance is key - it is a competitive industry so be prepared to work hard to land that role you want!

How do actors sabotage their careers?

There are lots of ways that actors can easily sabotage their career:

Not trying or being proactive enough. Giving up too easily. Not taking rejection well. You have to grow a thick skin in this industry and have lots of determination.

If you don't have professional headshot photos and showreel you will not be off to a good start.

Not rehearsing and practicing enough for your audition.

How many actors are on To Be Seen?

There are approximately 30,000+ actors registered on To Be Seen with hundreds more joining every week...

What trends have you noticed in casting?

Online auditions are becoming more common for the pre-audition phase. Casting directors are extremely busy and often work internationally so cannot actually be present at all auditions.

Should an actor ever do extra work?

When an actor is starting out on their career, it can be a useful to work as an extra.

By doing this the actor can earn some money and gain invaluable experience of being on a set.

Matt Damon and Ben Affleck once worked as extras and it didn't do their careers any harm!

Peter Chipping. Film Director and producer.

Peter is a very talented film director. Check out his work at http://peterchipping.co.uk/

Did you always want to be a director?

I guess so - although I started as an editor and that seemed a great role, like finishing a jigsaw puzzle from a large pile of disparate elements, many of which don't seem to join together. Then I realised I'd like to create those disparate elements myself, but not make them quite as disparate.

How did you get your start in the business?

I started in theatre and Yvonne Arnaud in Guildford, before enrolling at Ravensbourne for a new TV course, them got my first job at Central TV in Birmingham.

What was your big break?

Editing *Crossroads*.

What is your favourite thing about working in film?

Teamwork: No matter what ideas I get, there's always other people who can add to them and make them better.

And the least?

The gaps between projects.

What are you working on at the moment?

Three short interlocked comedies, two 60 minute broadcast documentaries and a feature paranormal thriller.

What is your favourite film?

The Conversation.

What mistakes do actors make at auditions?

Not showing the range of emotions that is available in their arsenal.

What projects are you hoping to get off the ground?

A feature paranormal thriller.

Favourite actress?

Michelle Pfeiffer in *The Fabulous Baker Boys*.

Jonathan Hansler and Clive Greenwood.

Jonathan and Clive have been acting for a long time and really know the industry. Everything there is to know about acting, these guys can tell you.

How To Be A Successful Actor. Becoming an Actorpreneur.

How did you two meet?

J: Clive and I met many moons ago, probably doing murder mysteries.

How do you collaborate?

J: Clive sits at the laptop, I make tea and pace around the room. We tend to have a good creative crossover as writers.

How did you get into acting?

J: Wandering round the garden at three years old dressed in a towel thinking I was Julius Caesar may have been a clue. It was all I was good at. I was crap academically. I went to a drama school which when I was there was very good but, due to two deaths a year later, closed. Maybe I should have retrained.

What advice would you give to actors who are not as established as you?

J: Unless you are serious about this business and would kill a relative to do it, get out. It is tough. On the lower rungs, it can be full of the biggest egotistical, untalented two-faced people. It gets a lot better as you get higher up. People are good at what they do and are generally nicer.

It is an industry that is not well policed, although generally we have a good union. If you are serious and have just murdered your uncle, network, meet people, go to festivals like Cannes, and blag it. Find a good agent, ask people about theirs, be versatile - although that may be a curse. Being excellent, and versatile at what you do, scares people off sometimes.

How do you think the industry has changed?

J: It's changed because films are made so incredibly cheaply today. Fifteen years ago, hundreds of people were queuing up to do one student film, for no money. It would cost a minimum of £250 an hour to edit a movie. Showreels were hugely costly. With the advent of technology and tiny broadcast quality cameras today, people can make a movie cheaply and quickly. There were of course no Casting Call Pro's or any other online services. There were just casting directors and answer phones.

If you did a show you would mail 10 x 8 photos with CV, SAE and flyer in a hard backed envelope. I did 97 fringe shows and spent 20 years before getting my first TV break via a play I blagged the auditions for (they wanted names) playing Peter Cook, so you can imagine what that cost me. Nowadays there are many ways of attracting attention via the internet.

What's next?

J: Well, we want to push *Cook & Moore* the movie and the play, and are probably going to do a reading of the film in front of an invited audience, including mates in the film industry. I have a couple of leads in features screening soon, and am shooting a feature a mate is directing in Jan as well as another in Malta in April/May. I am currently in *Decline and Fall* by Evelyn Waugh playing Dr Fagan, an eccentric headmaster, at the Old Red Lion with Sylvester McCoy till 29th Jan.

How To Be A Successful Actor. Becoming an Actorpreneur.

Samantha From Simon & How.

Samantha How is a brilliant agent. She has got me some amazing auditions and she knows pretty much everything about the industry. Read and learn. (but don't steal her)

What is the best way for an actor to approach an agent?

Agents have different requirements, but for us, emailing your CV and headshot, Spotlight page or performance invite is preferable to posting. Don't be too intimidated to call an agent and ask them how they prefer to be approached. That way you can only get it right!

What makes you take an actor on?

Predominantly talent and a gap in our client list for a particular type of actor. We'll initially watch a show-reel, look at a CV and headshot or spot someone in a showcase and invite them in for a chat. Once they've come to meet us first impressions are also key. Looking neat, being on time and being polite are so important. We'll potentially be sending these actors to casting directors who trust us so they are essentially our representatives as well as the other way round.

Describe an average day?

There's never nothing going on! Most of the day is taken up with us receiving 'breakdowns' for casting directors via phone or email and us making submissions, usually via Spotlight, direct email and by post. We also call casting directors following each submission (unless asked not to) to discuss the actors suggested. Around this we are organising auditions, normally for the next day, making sure actors have all the details they need including scripts and wardrobe instructions and booking actors in for jobs they have been confirmed for, organising wardrobe calls, pick-up time, contracts etc.

After working hours we are often busy attending performances or screenings our actors are in, going to showcases to spot new talent or hosting workshops with casting directors for our actors to attend.

Is there a lot of work out there?

There are periods when it goes a bit quiet, generally Christmas and around August, and the last year has been a tough one with arts cuts and a recession to deal with, but on the whole, there are always things going on. We have a wealth of growing talent in this country which has never been stronger and the entertainment industry isn't going anywhere. It is however getting ever more competitive out there so embarking on a career in acting isn't for the faint hearted. You need to prepare to work hard, be proactive and stay positive.

Is there still more work for men?

I'd say the actual work is fairly equal, but the competition for women is fiercer. A recent article in

How To Be A Successful Actor. Becoming an Actorpreneur.

The Stage said there are far more female applicants for positions on acting courses than males, with women accounting for two-thirds of applications to these courses. The ratio is roughly the same for applicants to technical theatre courses, where women also outnumber men two to one when applying. This is also certainly the case if you look at most agency websites where the female client lists are consistently larger than the male ones.

How often should an actor write to casting directors? What else can they do to help their career?

Please don't stalk them – it doesn't go down well! Write if you have something to say. If you've met them at a networking event, an audition, or a workshop, it's fine to follow up. If you know they are casting something you are right for either write to them or ask your agent to write on your behalf, highlighting why you're perfect for the role. Even if they've asked you to stay in touch, try to stick to professional contact. Letting them know you have new headshots, a new show-reel or inviting them to productions, for example.

Send emails during working hours and don't take it personally if you don't get a response.

What advice can you give to an actor who has just left drama school?

Research the people you're contacting, know who you are addressing, what do and what they've done in the past.

Make sure you're on Spotlight and keep your page as up to date as possible. If you can, upload show-reels and voice clips, make-sure your headshots are a good likeness and not years out of date. Keep your CV ordered, neat and up to date. Spotlight is where most submissions are made and where casting directors are most likely to see you first so it's vital you utilize it to its full potential.

Keep up to date on what's going on in film, theatre, TV and even advertising trends. It's important you know your industry and what's trending at any given time. Network whenever you have the opportunity.

Invite agents to come and see your work, but don't be offended if you don't get a response. We're a boutique agency and we can receive around 25 show invites in a day. Larger agencies and casting directors will be receiving a hell of a lot more. We all try to get out us much as we can but, unfortunately, can't get to everything. Don't be put off inviting again in the future if the opportunity arises.

Keep correspondence polite, concise and pay attention to spelling and grammar.

Don't rest on your laurels once you've graduated or found an agent. Be proactive, get out there and don't sit around waiting for the phone to ring. Take courses, workshops and attend seminars to keep learning and keep your skills sharp.

What is the best thing an actor can do for their career?

Do as much as you can to gain experience and knowledge. Do short films and take smaller roles to build up a show-reel and invest in great quality headshots. When you go to auditions make the effort. Be on time, be polite, learn the script if you've been given it and use the brief (a brief is a breakdown of the scene. Like a synopsis) if you have seen it. You're a professional and every audition is a job interview, so treat it as such. Network, network, network and most of all, stay positive.

And the worst?

Don't get angry or bitter if things get quieter. Do as much of the above as possible. Much more healthy and proactive!

Jane Frisby Interview

Jane Frisby is without a doubt one of the nicest people in the film industry. I met up with her to discuss a superb film she had just produced The Fighter's Ballad *and I have decided to put some of the interview in this book. We had a brilliant chat and anyone who wants to work in film or acting can learn something by listening to her advice.*

What made you want to go into producing?

I was getting a lot of low-to-micro budget film scripts, wanting the same commercial actors attached, either urban hoodie 'gangsta' films or Horror/Zombie type scripts, usually not very original or amazing.

I met Peter Cadwell putting *The Fighter's Ballad* on as a play. It received the Best of 5 Theatre Plays in the Independent Award, and the play was written by Peter Cadwell and his acting also got fantastic reviews, so the writing had already been much appreciated by critics and the public. Peter had already done the play to great success at the Actor's Church with great actor Jack Shepherd playing the Priest, but to a limited audience; it needed to go bigger. It had been done as a 'theatre piece already, and I put my producer's hat on. It just happened like that. It wasn't a conscious decision.

What was the hardest thing about making the film?

Getting the money... I started with wealthy friends that I knew, public funding, private investors and it just wasn't happening. Then luckily our Director Tony Ukpo's father, had investor contacts in Nigeria. That is where the money came from. We were very lucky.

Did you cast it?

Peter Cadwell was cast as he had written it, and is also a WONDERFUL actor, but I cast Clive [Russell] and all of the rest.

What drew you to the script?

It had so much to say. It's very relevant to life these days. The youth - what have they got now? Education isn't up to scratch, lack of work, mental health, people on the streets, violence, drugs.

Where do they channel that energy? The fact that this guy ends up in a church and has this confrontation with the Priest. It's controversial and asks questions of the audience and it challenges religion and the Church - there were so many issues I felt were very thought-provoking.

What was the initial first step?

First Step: there were actors who really loved the script, but were unavailable, Clive's agent called me and said he wanted to meet as he was interested. We all met him a few days later and he came on board the project, which was amazing news. That's how the project started.

How are you going to get it out there?

The easy part was shooting it actually! Then obviously the post-production, the colour grade, the sound, the music. Getting it out there has been very difficult. We went through the usual channels of trying to get into festivals, we did a BAFTA screening, which was fantastic - a good friend of mine managed to get BAFTA for half price. We invested in that and invited a lot of people. We also did a screening at Soho House and invited people to come.

The public response has been amazing. We put it up online and in the past few weeks we have had 600 people come to the website from all over the world. I am now looking at doing charity screenings - there are a lot of deserving charities out there - and religious screenings, going down that route. I want to do more screenings, as when the public sees it, it creates a lot of buzz. We are doing that as well as going down the normal route of sales agents.

Do you have any advice for people who want to make their own films?

Do it. Just do it. If you have a project and you feel like it should be made and you are passionate about it, then somehow you will get it done. Somehow, you will find a location you will get for nothing or cheap. Just get a group of people surrounding you who are as passionate as you are about it.

How hard was it to juggle doing the film and working as a casting director?

It has been very tough actually. There have been times when I have been pulling my hair out trying to get people to screenings. I didn't realise how hard it would be. Trying to work and do my job while casting a corporate or a commercial at the same time, whilst also looking after my daughter who is 15 has been a massive amount of balls being juggled. But sometimes you work well under pressure.

Would you ever want to direct?

Never. I love casting and I would love to do even more producing. I like working with actors whom I rate and having control of the project from script stage to final edit".

What made you choose the actors?

How To Be A Successful Actor. Becoming an Actorpreneur.

When I read the script I had a vision of someone like Liam Neeson. I also thought of the Priest as being a big man. I had a vision of this man being a mountain of a man, and he would be quite weathered because of his past. I have always remembered Clive from the RSC. He is a very subtle actor and also 6' 4" and big.

I think with him being Scottish as well, there is that sort of Celtic lilt to his voice. Talking to a fellow Scot. [**CB**: I'm a Scottish actor] Well, I'm not Scottish but I love Scottish actors, Irish actors - I have an apartment in Dublin - and the Welsh. The Scottish are great actors. There is something about Celts. The way the speak is just lyrical.

What changes have you noticed in the film industry?

The biggest change is the digital cameras. They have been absolutely massive and you can buy them for £1,000. We shot on the Canon 5D. It's a stills camera, but the quality is good for film. That has opened up a lot of people being able to make films. I think that is a good thing because it enables a lot of people with not a lot of money to make good quality films. The independent film making scene should be really buzzing now. The one thing I worry about is people trying to make indie films with little money, but trying to make them commercial as well.

What advice do you have for actors?

Learn as much as you can. Read screenplays, do workshops, go to master-classes, go to the theatre, go to the cinema, There are loads of social networking events you can go to. Watch other people's short films, especially if you really like the director. You never know where they are going to end up. That happened with me on a film that I did and I loved it.

A short film I cast got into the North London Film Festival and I got in touch with the director/ writer of this lovely short I saw there. Two years later, he got in touch and asked me to cast his short. It is social networking, keeping in touch with what's going on.

The first person to give me a commercial casting was Mel Smith. My dad had been around Soho handing out plastic Frisbees with *Jane Frisby Casting* on them. I got a phone call one evening and this guy said he was Mel Smith. He said., 'I am doing a commercial and I want you to cast it. I loved the Frisbee'. So I started working with Mel. It's things like that.

It's hard. There is a lot of work there for very little pay, but I think that is across the board - acting, casting, everything. I am casting this short with a wonderful director, Jack Price, who I have worked with many times in the past in Bristol. There is lots of talent there. I did that just for my train fare. It's not all about making money. If you are passionate and you want to work, you just have to keep doing it.

How To Be A Successful Actor. Becoming an Actorpreneur.

Unpaid acting work by Professionally Resting

*Professionally Resting is an actor in her late twenties who writes an amazing blog (*http://
professionallyresting.blogspot.co.uk/*) and also tweets (*https://twitter.com/ProResting*) about the
ridiculousness and unfairness of this industry we are in. Here is her opinion on unpaid acting work*

Expenses only.

Sadly this type of casting call is one that I'm all too used to seeing. At least 75% of castings will
contain the above sentence or a wonderfully inventive version of it (such as the incredible: 'This is
a no-pay experience!'). It's unfortunately become a fact of acting life and I've become as skilled at
sifting through castings as I have at rifling through sandwiches for rogue tomatoes. Directors will
try and soften the blow by telling you that you'll get a credit to put on your CV (gee, thanks) and
that they'll be providing you with food on set. On-set catering can be a thing of beauty (pizza) but it
can also be an utter horror made of stale sandwiches. Apparently actors can live on credits and
bread alone. If only landlords, phone companies and councils could be fobbed off in the same way.

Unpaid work has become a rather aggressive disease in the acting world. What was once the
domain of film students and wannabe film-makers has now entered the world of television. And this
is a worrying development. I understand that, however much they'd like to, students and smaller
production companies can't always afford to pay people. The ethics bother me because I believe
that if you can't afford to pay everyone then you probably shouldn't be making the piece in the first
place but that's an argument for another day. Unpaid work happens and sadly, just like the damp in
our flat, I have to deal with it for now and watch it ever so slowly ruin me. I should also admit that
I've taken on my fair share of unpaid work in the past. Unfortunately there are times when you have
very little choice and so you can either do nothing or take on some unpaid work in the hope that
it might just get you spotted. It won't, but you never know when that top agent is going to turn up
at a secondary school in Northampton to watch you prance about telling kids about the dangers of
heroin. But now the bigger companies have jumped on the bandwagon and suddenly everything is
starting to topple over.

There have been a string of very high-profile companies that have recently started advertising
unpaid or expenses only work. And when I say 'high-profile' I mean the type of companies
that produce widely watched prime time programmes that air on terrestrial channels. These
are companies that clearly have plenty of money, or at least enough cash to make sure that all
performers are fairly paid. When they start offering unpaid work, what kind of message does that
send out to all the other companies? Apparently it's now perfectly acceptable for these businesses
(one of whom made a profit of £471m last year) to get performers to work for free. But these
companies forget that actors often have a lot of time on their hands so it doesn't take too long
before they're outed via the beauties of social networking. But what happens when they get found
with their devious trousers around their tight-fisted ankles? Well, what has happened recently
is that they make like George Osborne and U-turn. However, they don't then promise to do the
honourable thing and actually pay actors. Oh no. Their reaction is to say that they will instead be
casting friends, family or employees. That's what this profession has been downgraded to. Actors
are now regarded so poorly that we can be instantly replaced with the make-up artist's cousin and

the focus puller's university mates the second we start to complain. We find ourselves so low on the career ladder that we've now been downgraded to the lackey that just holds the ladder and watches everyone else climb up it.

So what this means is that actors will yet again be forced into unpaid work as they desperately try to keep hold of a career that's more slippery than a greased-up seal. We continually find ourselves being held to ransom where we can either 'shut up and put up' or keep fighting and take the chance of never working again. Just like the next actor, I'd love the exposure that a prime time programme would offer but never at my own expense and certainly not just so an exec can save a few precious pennies and ensure that their bonus is intact for another year. Why should they get to go on exotic holidays when I'm left wondering how to survive for the next week on a tin of chopped tomatoes and a rapidly ageing nectarine? It's at its lowest, meanest level and until all actors make a stand against these companies, all we're doing is encouraging them to turn our already fragile industry into a laughing stock.

Jack Bowman

Jack Bowman is an amazing actor (he plays Jamie in my film Prose & Cons) and is also a director, writer and all-round brilliant guy who recently directed Stephen Fry. He also works for the Wireless Theatre Company and is the Associate Director of the Lost Theatre in London.

How did you break into acting?

Way back in the day, when I was a teenager, I won tickets to see a West End production called *Lust*, which starred Nigel Lawson and Sophie Aldred. I was absolutely blown away by it - it was a musical adaptation of *The Country Wife* at the Haymarket. After that, I was lucky enough to go backstage, meet Sophie and talk a little bit about what I'd just seen. It was just amazing. So, for once, I then agreed to go to the school play a few weeks later - a production of *Bugsy Malone* and, again, was blown away. So the following Monday, I joined the drama club and from there, did some am dram in South London, before setting off to University to study drama. And within a year of graduating, I got my Equity card and was working!

Did you find it easy?

Not at all, and I still don't. I don't think anyone does, successful or struggling. You really do need to love what you are doing and want to go forward and be prepared to adapt where needs be. Other careers might have a path. You could, for example, start out as a bus conductor, then become a garage manager, before rising to the head of transport in forty years. As an actor, that progression is never really your choice; it's luck, fate, luck, opportunity, luck... and a lot of luck.

How has the industry changed?

Weirdly, when I started out, a lot of agents advised me to get a second creative bow to help me stand out - I was asked, 'do you write, direct, anything like that?' Now, as I work as an actor, writer and director, I find a lot of industry people ask me, 'well, which are you?' I loosely classify myself now as a 'story-teller'; I can change my roles more fluidly, which also does cause a few eyebrows here and there. I think the biggest reason for this has been the expanding number of actors; casting directors often face overwhelming numbers of applications for a role - I think 5,000 is the average - so standing out to build relationships has remained the hardest part. Again, you have to love this career to want to do it!

What is the best advice you can give to an actor?

Keep reminding people that you're out there, that you're keen to work and, above all else, value yourself. It is so easy to work for free because we do what we do for art and love, yet the world needs that art and love so if you want to make a career of it, remember it is exactly that - a career. At the same time, never be closed off to any work offer... the correct answer to any approach is always, '*Maybe*'!

To train or not?

I certainly think you need an outside eye. I've known people come to acting late, or do it since they were five... I think the important point is always CONTINUE training. I remember thinking I left my course ready and fully formed. You're not. Find a good coach; I use Jeremy Stockwell who is a genius and I can rely on him to get the best out of anyone. Finding a good coach is exactly like finding a good agent; rare and special. Go to classes - in London alone there's the Actors' Centre, and the Actors' Guild, who are just amazing. I remember once I went to a class and was given the best advice I ever heard. Firstly, I was told, 'if someone comes to you and says, "Method acting is the only way forward", or "Meisner is the key", remember two words - 'snake oil', because what happens when you, as a Method actor, meet a Meisner actor? Learn, study and practice all disciplines. Secondly, when you take extra classes, don't pick the ones you'll enjoy, because you'll probably pick what you're good at. And if you're good at it, what's the point? It's great to keep skills fresh, but what about learning skills? Tightening up the areas where you're weaker? Keep pushing where you fail to make yourself a more rounded actor, and you'll be more castable.'

It's true - I realised then I'd, mostly, been attending classes for the things I found easy, so how was that going to improve my skills as an actor?

How do you get casting directors to notice you?

Attend workshops - these have exploded all over London in the last few years. Annelie Powell runs some excellent ones, as do Stand-Up Drama. You'll get good access to good people, and make sure you ask about how to follow it up and, more importantly, how you should approach that follow-up. If a casting director tells you face-to-face they don't like being emailed, then don't email them. But find a way to remind them you are still out there. Also remember, casting directors want you to make them look good, so if they get you in, they trust you. Make sure you know what they want - for example, one casting director might want you off book or knowing your side, whereas another won't see an audition as a memory test. And ask around - have any of your friends auditioned for this CD (actors call casting directors 'CD' for short)? What was their experience?

What is the most important thing an actor can do for their career?

Never, in any way, be a bad person. It is a very small world and bad-mouthing, bad behaviour, bad

How To Be A Successful Actor. Becoming an Actorpreneur.

anything gets heard very clearly and passed on very quickly. Be lovely to everyone.

What mistakes do actors make?

I think there's two relating to the above. Firstly, if you are unkempt, rude, bitchy and an arse to be with, socially or professionally, then it'll be game over, eventually. I would much rather work with people who are 80-90% as good as they could be but are lovely, rather than someone who gives 120% all the time, yet makes you feel awful to be around. Drop anyone who is constantly negative and unpleasant - there is saying, which I think is true, 'you're judged by the company you keep.' Keep good company.

Secondly, never let anyone undermine who you are or what you are worth - being an actor is a very noble profession and we have a very special responsibility; we entertain society when we all individually, want to forget our world. Without that release, that flight into a fantasy world for just a short time, we'd all go mad as a species.

Should an actor ever give up and do something else?

I refer to the words someone of whom I'll never be as great as - Sir Derek Jacobi. He summed it up brilliantly: 'You'll never be a master of your craft. But it you want to be an actor, stop. If you NEED to be an actor, never, ever give up.' And that's my problem: I need to be an actor!

Where it the best place to live as an actor?

For the UK? You'll always need to have a London base, but currently (as of 2014), also Manchester, Cardiff, Bristol and Belfast.

What is the main source of your work?

As I said before, I consider myself a 'story-teller' so, as a freelancer, I am able to look out for opportunities to write, direct, occasionally produce and act. I also work as a core member of The Wireless Theatre Company. The combination of all four really helps keep the wolf from the door. Currently, my main income has been from directing and producing, but these things have a habit of changing around. Fortunately, I can let them shift, provided I've done some acting!

What's next for you?

2013? Finishing *The Springheel Saga* (Series 2 and 3 are released this year), with a *Making Of...* special on that too; the release of *Prose and Cons,* pitching to Radio 4 through Wireless, several radio and audio ideas, writing a screenplay, directing a sequel to *We Are The BBC* (which starred Stephen Fry) and I've just been offered an acting role in February. And maybe a return trip to Minneapolis this year - after Series 1 of *Springheel* won the Ogle, they've been asking us to return for this year's event, so who knows...

Finally, to those reading this book, I'd like to say one thing. Remember to be bright, happy and supportive, because one day, we may meet. And I may have heard about you first. And to steal from Jeremy Stockwell, 'Be light of heart and play freely!'

How To Be A Successful Actor. Becoming an Actorpreneur.
(Jack is now also the associate director of the Lost Theatre)

Leoni Kibbey

Leoni Kibbey is a casting director, producer and actor. She also started and runs the St Alban's Film Festival. I have worked with her a few times and she is brilliant.

How did you get into acting?

I was blessed with creative, ambitious, intelligent parents and three siblings. As a family we loved to play games (card games/board games/puzzles/outdoor games/rounders). I guess acting is just an extension of my love of 'playing'. My Mum is a jazz singer. We lived for a while in the Lake District and used to watch her at Sunday lunchtime jazz shows, I was in awe. I was a bit of a shy introverted child, Mum was a bit concerned until she came to see me sing in school and said I came alive. My first taste of theatre was in a local production of *The Sound of Music* at the age of 7 - playing Gretel, my audition was the speech at the end of Michael Jackson's *Thriller*: 'darkness falls across the land etc..'. I think they thought it was weird but cute. I adored the process then, the buzz of being backstage and being given the responsibility of learning lines. I wasn't a 'starlet', even at a young age I took my work seriously as well as, of course, having a massive load of fun behind the scenes. (Nothing changed there). I was always involved in local theatre groups growing up and after A-levels went to Mountview Theatre School. That was 12 years ago now. Tempus Fugit.

How do you manage to juggle a successful acting career with being a successful casting director?

Let's just say life is intense. I work a LOT. I like to be busy and I think my careers complement each other and give me a good insight into the industry. I am a creative person as well as a business woman. In terms of how I mentally and physically manage it? The pressure can get to me, especially whilst trying to be the best mum to my daughters. I do sometimes feel like I am working three full time jobs and have to keep a check on my physical and mental health and listen to when my body needs to rest. I try to squeeze in some exercise into my schedule and I take time out doing things I love and seeing people I love. Some people say there may come a point when I will have to choose between my careers but in the words of my Mother, 'Don't let anyone tell you that you can't do something' and, right now, both careers are working for me. The casting helps provide a good life for me and my girls and any acting roles I take are a total bonus.

What do you love about your job?

I am my own boss and can be in control of my own career and time. I get to be creative. I meet loads of lovely people. Every day is different. One of the directors I work with always brings a huge bag of Skittles to meetings...

How To Be A Successful Actor. Becoming an Actorpreneur.

Do you have any advice for actors?

Never get bitter, particularly about your agent. Be proactive, be positive. Work very very *very* hard. Get a showreel. If you stop enjoying it then don't do it. Do email me but as I get hundreds of emails a week from actors I can't usually reply but I do look at all emails. Sounds cheesy but be true to yourself. Networking is great but don't force things - better to be friendly than to seem desperate. You get out what you put back in. Always go with your gut instinct. Don't get cosmetic surgery. Floss. Use Sunscreen.

What's next?

I'm constantly asking myself that. I've been offered a nice acting role in the feature *Jack The Ripper, Whitechapel 1888* playing Mrs Swanson, the lead detective's wife. I've co-written a short film for which I am trying to pull some funding together. I've just booked myself a session to record a new voice reel, and I am casting commercials, a Channel 4 shoot and several feature films at various stages of development . The most recent film I have taken on is a feature adaptation of an award winning novel and I'm tying up casting for *Sure Fire Hit*, the British Action Movie with Chris Noth (Mr Big from *Sex & The City*). However I've just realised I'm taking my daughters on a much needed holiday to Disneyland Paris during the premiere of SATC2 so won't be attending that!

Is it harder for women?

YES. Mainly due to statistics of there being more women acting. But I don't think about it because you can make up a thousand excuses for why your career isn't going the way you want it to go.

What does your average day consist of?

Wake up, give kids my full attention, get them ready for school, school run, pop to a morning exercise class, back to the office at home - calls, emails. Sending out offers, chasing agents. A client may call with a new breakdown for a commercial or stills shoot, or perhaps to discuss a new feature. Send out the breakdown, stick a load of washing in the machine, cuppa, snack, tidy myself up and dash into London for meetings, reading a script/answering emails on the blackberry while on the way to London, meetings.. maybe a quick commercial casting as an actress, sometimes I'm back in time to collect the kids at 4pm and then take my business calls/send emails while making their tea. Homework. And then kids' bath and bed - stories. This is my favourite time of day when we relax and I get to read their favourite books like *Charlie and the Chocolate Factory*. Then it's back to the computer to review suggestions for my breakdown, the calls to the US to chase offers on feature films, update my acting CV, watch *Glee*, print off my short film script and make some edits, have a chat to some friends online/phone. (Or often I stay in London for showcases, screenings or networking events) .. plan the next day, play a bit of the latest *Professor Layton* on the DS or read a bit of my book and then crash.

Did having children affect your career in any way?

Yes. In a very positive way. They gave me back my focus.

Miki Yamashita Interview

Miki is a very talented actor, an opera singer and a really funny person. (http://www.mikiyamashita.com/)

What made you go into acting?

I think I was interested in the arts and performing even before I was aware of it. My mother says that as a child, I danced and sang around the house so much that she put me in lessons as soon as I was old enough, because she wanted me to learn how to do it right. My parents are both teachers, so their solution for everything is education. It's actually a pretty good philosophy. As I grew conscious of my passions in life, I consistently made life decisions that propelled me towards a life as a performing artist. Let's just say I never gravitated towards coal-mining.

Could you ever do anything else?

I guess the right answer is that I actually do many other things. Having spent my life around many other actors, I have observed that I may be a slightly different breed than most. I have a group of actor friends that I started out with performing improvisation and sketch comedy with at Walt Disney World, who are still doing only that; I have another group who I did a lot of musical theatre with, who are still focusing only on Broadway; same with opera people and comedy writers and commercial actors and episodic television actors. I am really lucky in that I am actively able to book work in all of these areas, and I consider that huge spectrum of interests to be my pursuit as a whole, so if my universe is that huge, understandably there really isn't an 'anything else' for me.

You famously said: 'If this business kills me, it will be after everyone in it has my headshot.' That's a go-getting attitude that can be missing in a lot of performers. Do you agree?

My dear friend Bonnie Gillespie was kind enough to include that in her brilliant book, *Self-Management for Actors*. When a newer edition came out, she asked if she could include it again, and I said of course, except that I didn't want to imply that manically blanketing an acting market with headshots was the technique I was espousing. I believe in being fiercely motivated, but in a very focused and strategic manner. There's a young actor in LA, I haven't seen him in a while, but this crazy kid literally plastered the exterior of his car with his headshots. I swear! He drives around in this car all day long hoping for, I don't know, to get pulled over by a casting director and get asked to do a monologue by the side of the road? I don't know! But it's pretty delusional and highly misguided. I guess what I meant to say is that, 'If this business kills me, it will be after everyone in it whom I have researched and targeted as potential buyers for my product has my headshot.'

Over the years, I have met so many actors; some have almost zero motivation and ambition to do the basic work that is necessary to even have a chance at success; others are rabidly foaming at the mouth and doing everything they can desperately and inefficiently so that they can get ahead. What I've learned from these actors is that there is a better way, there is a sweet spot, where you have a calm, cool, focused energy that propels you forward slowly, steadily, and intelligently. Wow, I think this is officially the most Asian thing I have ever said!

I find you incredibly funny, has your sense of humour helped you survive in showbusiness? Is it possible to do this without one?

Thank you! I think it's literally impossible not to develop a sense of humour as a professional actor. I was once asked to sing opera while running full speed on a treadmill in a sequinned gown. I was once told to continue reciting my monologue while the casting director got on her cell phone and ordered a chicken salad. I was once physically threatened by a male chorus dancer. I mean, as actors, this is daily life, okay? And I think if you don't find it hilarious, you become seriously mentally damaged in a way that prevents you from functioning in society as a normal adult. And then it becomes this wonderful tool to help you consistently cope with the vast array of indignities that actors face all the time.

What's the hardest thing about being an actor?

The hardest thing about being an actor is when Chanel sends you so much free couture from their latest collection that you run out of assistants to re-gift them to. JUST KIDDING!!! That's what most people think actors' problems are. The general public is fed nothing but lies about our profession, and they are only provided with the success narrative. It's part of the machine that allows the industry to maintain its operations, so you have to accept that civilians are never going to get what most of us go through. The most difficult thing is really how seldom we are actually able to do our work, and that we must spend an inordinate amount of time doing work that has nothing to do with performing in order to bankroll the pursuit of our REAL work.

And the best?

The best thing about being an actor is getting to crash your car into an 18-

wheeler, blaming it all on your assistant, and showing up 4 hours late to set where they will still tell you you're the perfect choice to play Liz Taylor. HA HA HAAA. Seriously, the best thing about this profession is that we are constantly challenged to imagine what is possible. Every time I get an audition, whatever it is, a commercial where I'm a pretty Asian mom, or an opera where I'm a flying ghost bird-spirit, or a daytime drama where I'm the secretary to the family patriarch, I get to make decisions about these characters based on my imagination, my life experience, and what is on the page. And no one else is going to make the same set of choices that I will. Even if I don't get the part, for a brief moment, for the duration of that audition, my humanity was merged with that character, and I find great fulfilment in my ability to execute that with consistency and quality.

What is your favourite thing that you have worked on?

My favourite thing that I have worked on is an original new work in which I sang a principal role, with Los Angeles Opera. The piece was called *The White Bird of Poston*, and it was newly commissioned specifically for the purposes of educational and community outreach in the city of Los Angeles. The opera is about the Japanese American Internment during World War II, a very dark part of American history. The music and the story are so beautifully written, I felt so honoured to be a part of it, and I felt like it used so many of my skills simultaneously — my classically trained voice, my acting training, my dance training, and even a little bit of my abilities as a comedienne. And on top of that, it had such profound cultural significance to me as a Japanese American.

You have a great niche as an actress: you studied opera, has this greatly helped your acting career or is it separate thing?

As I mentioned earlier, there are a lot of people that I started out with, training and performing professionally as serious classical or musical theatre singers, who are still completely focused on only that sector of performance. For me, singing eventually became something glamorous and glorious that I could just keep hidden in my back pocket, and whip it out suddenly and just stun people with it as needed. This evolution mostly took place because I moved from the New York acting market which is very heavily theatre-based, to Los Angeles, which of course focuses much more on, well, speaking and not singing. But even without the move, I think I was really adamant about transcending musical theatre; I felt that I had more to accomplish in other areas, and my interests had a much wider span than just singing in musicals until I was dead.

Advice for actors?

My advice for actors is pretty depressing, but realistic. If at all possible, get a degree in a subject that has nothing to do with drama or music. I've made

How To Be A Successful Actor. Becoming an Actorpreneur.

a lot of hideous mistakes in life, but the one thing I did right was to earn a college degree in English literature instead of acting or vocal performance. Even though many would say a degree in English is almost as useless, I would have to argue otherwise. The acting business becomes more and more competitive every day, and what sets me apart from many others is my relentless desire to articulate my own experience. As a writer, I have a heightened sense of power because for the most part, words on a page cannot be refused or rejected because the writer isn't blond or skinny. I am shut out of thousands of performing job opportunities a day simply because of my physical appearance, something that cannot be transformed by 'working hard.' Trust me, I've tried. Exercising cannot change your race!

So my advice is to find tangible skills that will enable you to support your pursuit of acting for a very *very* long time.

But ultimately, have faith that you are answering a divine calling by being an artist. And know that you are in control of what you choose to sacrifice for this calling.

What's next for you?

I'm about to make big changes to my online presence; a fellow LA actress, Sarah Sido, taught me a lot about building websites, so I'm going to use those skills to rebrand my personal page, as well as start a blog about acting. Wow, now I've said it so I better do it!

Favourite actors

I think my favourite male actor is Jim Carrey. A lot of my earlier sketch comedy and improvisational work I did at Walt Disney World was heavily influenced by him, and I have deep respect for his significant capabilities as a dramatic actor. He is so interesting to watch doing anything! Let's say if, starting tomorrow, he stopped making studio feature films and decided to just host a vegan cooking show on HGTV, I would watch that.

For female actresses, I would rather be executed than name just one. Meryl Streep seems to literally becomes other human beings, to the point where it actually scares me. Meryl is a frightening example of sheer mastery of the craft. I would like to see her play some kind of deep sea creature or something, because that lady would seriously prepare for the role by eating paramecium and withstanding 500 bars of atmospheric pressure. And that's entertainment, my friends.

I love Julianne Moore's work, because I find that no matter who she plays, her characterization is so detailed and complete that I feel like I actually live out the movie in real time as her role. The performance is so intimate and honest and infused with inner life that I feel like I AM her character. Believe me, it takes skill to convince a short Asian girl that she is a white 1950s housewife.

How To Be A Successful Actor. Becoming an Actorpreneur.

Andrew Tiernan

I had the pleasure of working with one of Britain most hard working and talented actors, Andrew Tiernan, on Jason Croot's film Le Fear, Le Sequel. He was kind enough to give me an interview, and it's a stunner. This is a guy who really knows what he is talking about.

You are in *Prisoners' Wives* the new BBC Drama, what was it like working on that?

All credit to the production as they took a risk with me, as usually I'm the Bad guy, so this time I'm on the other side of the law playing DS Hunter who is investigating the murder that Gemma's (Emma Rigby) husband Steve (Jonas Armstrong) has been accused of. The directors and producers wanted an edge to this guy and they knew I could bring that to the role, which was great for me. I had to get my head into Cop mode, as I haven't done that for a very long time, in fact since *Prime Suspect* when I was a young copper with Helen Mirren and Tom Bell. Hopefully I've done a good job. But that was easy as Julie Geary's writing is fantastic.

You played Ephialtes, in Zack Snyder's *300*, how did you manage to put in such a good performance under all of that prosthetic?

It's great because you don't get recognized. I have always tried to transform myself for each role. The prosthetics was like a mask that I could manipulate with my facial muscles, but I had to exaggerate my expressions to move the inch thick prosthetic. I enjoy mask work, so that wasn't the hardest thing for me to do. When you're trying to transform yourself without the use of prosthetics, that is the challenge. I've fluctuated my weight and appearance over the years to fit the roles, I was influenced by Robert De Niro when he put a ton of weight on for *Raging Bull* but it's quite a dangerous thing to do and not everyone in the business appreciates it, some have thought that I've just let myself go, so I doubt I'll be putting on the pounds again anytime soon, unless it is under prosthetics.

You are a successful actor, but still do your own projects, why?

It's all about the work. It's what I've always wanted to do. I wanted to have some kind of control over my work at some point. What people forget is that it's the writer and producers who are in control. We can only perform what is written on the page. And when we're not doing those jobs, we're waiting around for work, it can send most actors insane, so I try to keep myself busy between jobs.

Tell us about the short film you've recently directed; *Flush.*

Flush came about after the writer; Kevin O'Donohoe, told me about an experience he had with some estate agents. One of the estate agents asked to use the toilet in his flat and was in there for an unexpectedly long time and managed to stink the place out. He thought that the guy had done it deliberately, so he decided to get his own back and came up with this very funny little script. We made it independently; I got Shona McWilliams and Simon Balfour in to help me produce it. We've

How To Be A Successful Actor. Becoming an Actorpreneur.

just finished post-production and we've entered it into some film festivals We're very excited about it. We're planning to do some feature films later in the year with the same production team and a new script by Kevin called *UK18,* a political drama set in the near future.

How did you get started as an actor?

I was into films from an early age and would visit the local cinema on my own, The Grove. I'd watch all the Ray Harryhausen adventures and then I managed to see some of Peter Bogdanovich's films, such as *Paper Moon* and *What's up Doc?.* So I suppose the bug started there, and eventually I decided it was something I wanted to do as a career. I started working at the Midlands Art Centre after joining the Youth Theatre there, then ended up at the Drama Centre London.

Who/what is your inspirations?

If you'd asked me a few years ago, I would have said De Niro and Scorsese, but I think really it is people like Powell and Pressburger, Nicholas Roeg, Lindsay Anderson and Ken Russell who inspire me, and always have. I also have an admiration for Polanski's films, one of the very first films I remember seeing was *Repulsion* when it was screened on television and it freaked me right out.

What is your favourite film?

At the moment, I would have to say it's Ken Russell's *The Boy Friend.* It was such a shock when he passed away, but I had managed to finally get the film on DVD the week before his passing. And it's just as wonderfully spectacular as when I first watched it, what a genius. But there are so many films that I love, that I have a top 40 in my head every week. Though there are certain ones that always top the list and not necessarily everyone's favourites.

How has the industry changed for actors?

Since I joined the industry rather a lot has changed. When I first started there was a lot more opportunities and a lot more drama was made for TV. But also there were a lot more theatre companies; we thought cuts were bad back then, but now it's unbelievable. But on a positive note, technology has improved such that artists can develop and produce their own independent work a lot more easily than back then. And it's possible for that work to be seen in different markets.

What are your opinions on reality TV?

Unfortunately, I think that it's had a knock on effect in our industry and not just the fact that there's not enough drama being produced, but reality TV is very cheap for the networks to produce and people seem to want to watch it. It's a very sad time, as I think that when we look back at this period, we will think: where were the great British TV Drama Writers that we used to produce like Alan Bleasdale, Dennis Potter or Peter McDougall? The networks should really pump more of the money they make from this cheap stuff into quality writing and drama, instead of squeezing the budgets. But we as artists can't rely on them anymore, we have to do it ourselves if we have a story to tell and find our own ways to distribute it.

What do you think of celebrity culture? What harm does it do?

Recently I was having a conversation with a young actor and we were chatting about the business and I mentioned that I'd worked with Simon Callow, the renowned theatre actor and writer. He must have misheard me, as suddenly he shrieked in excitement 'You know Simon Cowell!?!' I can forgive him for not knowing who Simon Callow is, but that reaction to the possibility that I could introduce him to Simon Cowell was deeply concerning. And I am seeing it more and more. Actors who manage to get themselves roles on productions and the next step for them is a celebrity dance show or the jungle one. Shows where you have swallow things in order to gain more celebrity status. How ironic is that!? I think what this culture of celebrity has done has made some people very ignorant and obsessed with materialistic things. I think what will happen is when people think back to the noughties, no one will be remembered for any kind of art or music, the era will be remembered for the wars that took place and the banking crisis. And just for the record, I don't know Simon Cowell.

What next?

We are going to change things.

Links:

IMDb: http://www.imdb.com/name/nm0862907/
Official Website: http://web.mac.com/andytiernan/Andrew_Tiernan

Professionally Resting Interview.

The talented actor behind the blog Professionally Resting first caught my eye on Twitter. She is brave, witty and accurate about the downside of the acting industry. As an actor myself I just read her tweets/blog posts and nod. I just had to interview her, so here it is. I also have a guest article from her above.

What made you start your blog?

I'd been reading a few other acting blogs online and I soon realised that none really covered what it's like to be an actual working actor. Many are written by actors who are constantly in work and that was something that I just couldn't really identify with. Most actors I know spend a great deal of their time resting and I wanted to create something fun and supportive for those of us that regularly find ourselves within the unemployed majority. I also wanted to use it as an excuse to keep busy. There are days when there's very little work coming in and having a blog to think about really keeps me feeling like I'm at least doing something creative.

Tell us a bit about yourself (without giving too much away)!

It's always tough answering these questions without sounding like you're on *Blind Date*! I'm in my late twenties and have been acting (on and off) since graduating from drama school in 2006. I had a break for a couple of years after getting a bit trapped in a temping job that became permanent. It was a horrible job but it meant I could have a couple of years actually earning money and being able to buy things that had previously been a luxury like food that isn't on the reduced shelf. However, there's nothing quite like a miserable job to remind you exactly what it is that you really want to be doing and that was the catalyst to making me find acting work again so that I could finally escape.

What do you think of the acting industry?

It's very much a love/hate relationship. I regularly complain about it on Twitter and on my blog because it honestly drives me insane. It can feel that it often has more to do with luck than talent and you are completely at the mercy of those in control of the work that is out there. It often feels like many companies and channels operate a closed shop policy and I think many of them are guilty of working with the same very tiny gang of actors time and time again. I read an article recently that said there was a very small pool of talent out there which simply isn't true. There's an absolute ocean of clever and gifted people out there but they often get ignored as there are other names and faces that are deemed more popular. Unfortunately viewing figures and ticket sales are placed about creating quality work and while I accept that many of those performers that are used time and time again are very good at what they do, a bit of variety really wouldn't go amiss! However, having said that, these are the very industries that would pay you a month's rent to mess around as a time-travelling police officer for the day and that's why I'm still slogging away at it!

What is the worst casting you have ever seen?

There are so many to choose from! The reason I started tweeting about castings was because people were so shocked at just how insulting and offensive and downright baffling they often were. Ones such as 'No pay unfortunately but you will get to ride in a white stretch limo with a midget and the band' and 'She looks a bit like a trollop but tries to dress a bit classy' have been incredible finds. However, I think the worst has to be one that I saw recently asking for actors to play characters in a sweatshop and the company (a very well-known TV channel) were only offering expenses. I thought I was past being shocked by castings but this one was offensive on so many levels that I genuinely had to keep re-reading it just to make sure that I was seeing it properly. Sadly I was.

What was the catalyst behind you starting your blog?

111

How To Be A Successful Actor. Becoming an Actorpreneur.

As I said, it was because I felt like I couldn't relate to the other acting blogs out there and I felt that there needed to be a voice that represented normal working actors who often find themselves out of work. However, although I knew that it was something I wanted to do, it took me a while to actually get it started. It only happened when I was coming back on the train after a month performing at the Edinburgh Festival. I'd stupidly forgotten to bring a book and my boyfriend and I were unable to sit together so to keep myself occupied, I just started writing. After nearly 4 hours of solid writing, I realised I had a lot to say on the subject of acting and after a bit of encouragement from my boyfriend who's also a blogger, the blog was born.

What can be done to improve the kind of roles women get?

It has to start with the writing. There is not a day goes by that I don't see at least one casting where a woman is required to either be a stripper or a prostitute and although I often make a joke of it on Twitter, it is very worrying too. There is such great writing out there for men but female roles are so often overlooked. So many times I read castings where all the male characters are given weird and wonderful characteristics while the women are just written to look nice. There are some incredible writers out there who are really trying to make sure that there are strong, interesting roles for women but they need support from the major producers for their work to get made and seen. I do think that it's changing and television and film is starting to listen but it feels like a very slow process that needs to speed up a little!

What is your favourite, and least favourite, thing about the industry?

Let's start with my least favourite and get the negative stuff out the way. It has to be the lack of good, paid work out there for actors. So many companies expect actors to work for free and although I completely understand how difficult it must be working on a tight budget, it's tough when you're faced with it day after day. Acting is something that I stupidly want to do for the rest of my life but it's hard when people seem to think that by offering you a limp cheese sandwich and £5 to cover your travel expenses, they're doing you a favour. I've done jobs in the past where I've essentially been paying to be part of them and that's when you know that something has gone wrong.

And my favourite thing about the industry? It's that you just don't know what's coming up next. A few months ago I was whinging on Twitter about how there didn't seem to be any work out there and literally minutes later, my agent was on the phone with an audition for an incredible part in a feature film. I didn't get the role but I do love how your luck changes from one minute to the next. Although it can be pretty unnerving at times, especially when you're going through a particularly quiet spell, it's incredibly exhilarating too. I think it's a little bit addictive which is why actors put themselves through such torment.

You blog and tweet under a pseudonym, do you believe it would harm your acting career if you didn't? Can you be critical?

How To Be A Successful Actor. Becoming an Actorpreneur.

The decision to write under a pseudonym was made so that I could be openly critical about the industry. As an actor you have to be so careful because you never know who you're going to be working with next and I think that means a lot of actors are worried about speaking out about how infuriating this industry can be. Writing anonymously gives me the freedom to be brutally honest about the problems I face without jeopardising my acting career. Although there are days when I wish I could just tweet under my real name, I'm sure I'd have been in a fair bit of trouble for some of my comments, especially about casting calls and auditions.

What was your favourite ever job?

Despite going on about getting paid, my favourite job was one when I didn't receive a penny. It was one of the first jobs I did after graduating from drama school and was a devised piece. It was pretty shambolic most of the time and we didn't even get expenses but it was incredible experience seeing a project from the first meeting where we had some terrible ideas to the final night of performance. We barely sold any tickets (mainly because it was listed incorrectly meaning that most audience members turned up about 5 minutes before it was about to end) but it was great fun and a real learning curve for me as a new actor.

... and your least?

A summer-long Shakespeare festival. It was fun for about a fortnight but after three months away from home on only £25 a week, I was in a state. The plays were performed outdoors and it was a particularly bad summer which meant that we spent a lot of time performing in soaking wet velvet dresses. British audiences are incredibly resilient and would determinedly sit there huddled up in anoraks and shelter under umbrellas while we battled with wind, rain, thunder and lightning. Because I was earning so little money, I was mainly living off value bran flakes and tomato soup so I ended the three months malnourished, exhausted, utterly sick of the sight and sound of Shakespeare and with about £4 in my bank account. That was something they really didn't warn me about in drama school!

You can read the Professionally Resting Blog here: http://professionallyresting.blogspot.co.uk/ Follow her on Twitter too. She's funny.

Felicity Jackson, founder of Surviving Actors Interview.

Felicity Jackson has been known in the acting industry for years now thanks to her awesome Surviving Actors convention. This year she also came to the attention of Alan Sugar, becoming one of his apprentices. She gives us the gossip on business, acting and her apprentice experience.

What was the idea behind Surviving Actors?

How To Be A Successful Actor. Becoming an Actorpreneur.

Surviving Actors was a initially going to be a recruitment fair for actors to find those 'in between' jobs. We then added the two other key areas to the event - Develop and Create. We believe that all three areas are important to a successful career!

How did you make Surviving Actors a success?

Surviving Actors was a success from our first event because I made sure that I spoke to as many actors as I could to form an event that would be useful to all those involved. We also gained support from Fourth Wall Magazine who were a huge help with our website and marketing.

The last Surviving Actors was a resounding success, everyone I knew was there, how does that feel?

It was an incredible feeling - the event doubled in size, and the response was phenomenal. It definitely inspired me to carry on running my events and to work on what I have already achieved.

What is your background?

I went to Drama School to train as an actress which I enjoyed immensely. After graduating I was fortunate to work in a couple of tours, and also did various 'in between' jobs which is where I gained a lot of my contacts that I share with the Surviving Actors visitors. I then came up with the idea to set up my own business, and now that is what I do full time!

What is the most important thing you have learned in business?

I've learnt that in order to maintain a successful business you must build good relationships with other similar companies who are at the same stages - you really can help each other out!

What is the most important thing an actor can do to help their career?

I believe that planning for those 'in between' times is extremely important - finding well paid work that utilises your acting skills. I also believe in taking chances, putting your own work on and not sitting back and waiting for the phone to ring!

How was your Apprentice experience?

Wow - it's hard to summarise it in just one sentence! It was a crazy and surreal experience, but I

How To Be A Successful Actor. Becoming an Actorpreneur.

loved every second of it! The board room is pretty scary - no amount of auditions can every prepare you for those nerves! I was inspired by the other candidates I worked with, and learnt from all the tasks I was involved in! My favourite point was when we were doing the graphic design for 'Ampi Apps' - it was refreshing to use my creative skills!

How can companies get involved with Surviving Actors?

Companies can become involved by checking out the dates of our next convention and exhibiting there. It's a great chance to meet actors who could benefit from the services that they offer. The day is well thought out, and always keeps the actors needs at the fore front of every decision. It's created by actors, for actors!

What's next?

The next Surviving Actor convention. You can register for a free e-ticket here : http://survivingactors.com/register.html

[Note: Felicity Jackson now works for Starnow]

Paul Burton, Ronnie Le Drew and Leoni Kibbey Interview.

As an actor, continual training is important. So I have interviewed Paul Burton, Ronnie Le Drew and Leoni Kibbey who do masterclasses for proactive actors at the famous Elstree Studios.

Paul Burton

What's your background?

Gosh, that could take hours to explain! I have twenty-two years of experience running a variety of my own theatre, film, TV and radio projects. I'm basically a self-employed writer, filmmaker and film andTV historian.

How important is it for actors to keep training?

I think it is very important. I personally believe each of the masterclasses which we are holding will benefit actors and actresses (yes, despite being only 37, I am old fashioned and still use both titles!) a great deal. I think learning new skills is also essential in this industry. As a director I am always more impressed when I get an application for an actor or an actress who has shown to continue to take extra training and learn new skills post drama school. It shows that they are hardworking and serious about their careers in what is obviously a very competitive world.

How To Be A Successful Actor. Becoming an Actorpreneur.

Is it exciting to be at Elstree studios?

Yes, so many of my favourite films have been made at the complex since 1924, so to be walking down the same corridors and using the same rooms and areas used by my favourite actors, actresses, producers and directors is a great thrill. I never tire of walking through the gates and entering the studios. And the management have been so supportive to me over the last few years.

Leoni Kibbey

Tell me about the masterclass

I was really pleased to be asked by Paul Burton to teach on his masterclass sessions. He runs a variety of masterclasses for actors and actresses which are taken by experienced professionals from the world of theatre, film and television at Elstree Studios, in Hertfordshire.

What will you be teaching at the masterclasses?

I am teaching three different day long courses - each day will be fun and practical, there will be lots of chances to perform and get involved. I am certainly more 'get up and do' than 'sit down and listen'. One of the classes is a casting masterclass just for women and then there are two for anyone age 18+: a screen acting day and an audition technique day. I think having an understanding of the industry is as important as talent and these masterclasses will help develop both as well as give you an opportunity to practise your skills and receive honest constructive feedback.

I often run casting workshops which last just a couple of hours. I am looking forward to giving a more intense day long workshop as it gives the actors a chance to learn more and to totally immerse their day in the world of casting as well as for me to learn more about them as actors and actresses.

I think they are very good value and having lunch included is an added bonus. For full details on the courses go to the masterclass website:

As an actor yourself, what do you think the benefits of continual training are?

It keeps your skills honed. It keeps you fresh as an actor. It allows you to make contacts and meet new people. I think a workshop session is a great way to learn because by watching others you also get a good measure of your own ability and what you may need to work on as well as learning from others.

How To Be A Successful Actor. Becoming an Actorpreneur.

How do you think the masterclasses will help people in their career?

It will give them a better awareness of the industry and how to approach work and auditions. It will give them pointers on how to improve their acting and I think any opportunity to meet a casting director is another step closer towards getting a job. In this relaxed, fun environment it will hopefully allow people to show the best of their talent throughout the day.

What is your background?

I trained as an actress at Mountview Theatre School, graduating in 1998. Since then I have worked as an actress, casting director and now producer. I am a busy multi-tasker and I understand all aspects of the industry and I enjoy passing that on in a workshop setting. I now regularly cast commercials and TV projects and feature films - including the multi-million pound feature film *Shakespeare's Daughter* which I am about to begin casting.

Ronnie Le Drew

Tell me about the masterclass

I was asked by Paul Burton to run a day's masterclass on puppet manipulation. we talked about how many students, time for Q&A and an opportunity for showing clips from my professional work over many years, all this and lunch too! Of course the answer was Yes.

What will you be teaching at the masterclasses?

The day will begin with a short introduction, and then straight into the manipulation of Glove Puppets, Rod Puppets and Marionettes (String puppets). Each of the different kind of puppet requires an individual skill which I intend to pass on to the students. Learning all this will take more than a day's course, but I hope to leave knowing that each student will have a knowledge of the basic performance possibilities of each puppet.

As an entertainer yourself, what do you think the benefits of continual training are?

I am a puppeteer first with some acting skills, the benefits of continual training are the same for both actor and puppeteer. Learning new skills only enhances your knowledge and opens your eyes to new opportunities, which can only be a good thing for both an actor and

puppeteer. You never stop learning, to do so will inhibit your
professional career.

How do you think the masterclasses will help people in their careers?

I hope to add to the actor/performer new skills which in today's
theatre, film and television, is essential. Actor/performers are
regularly asked what else can you do other than act!

What is your background?

I started as an apprentice puppeteer at the Little Angel Theatre
way back in the 60s and went on to work in Television Film For more
information do see my web page :-
www.ronnieledrew.com

What is your speciality?

My speciality is performing, directing, and teaching Puppetry in
all its forms. It has been my profession for all my working career
and continues to give me tremendous pleasure.

When Ronnie Met Zippy, the utterly splendid biography of Ronnie Le Drew, out now.

Elliot Grove, Founder of Raindance, Interview.

*I took a course with Elliot Grove years ago. His knowledge of film and film-making is vast and
impressive. Every actor, writer and director should take a course or go to the awards.*

When did you start Raindance and what was the premise behind it?

I started Raindance in 1992 as way to make contacts in the film industry. I started bringing over
well-known tutors from America. The response was astounding, and within a few months, British
film-makers started making films again. So I thought I'd start a film festival in the heart of London
in the week before the now-defunct MIFED market, because I noticed a lot of acquisition execs
hanging out at the Meridian Hotel on their way to MIFED in Milan.

I then learned a very painful lesson about British culture. The British, unlike my native Canadians,
are very snobbish - and as they couldn't see a government logo or brand on my poster assumed I
was just another tourist. I was pretty much wished bad luck by everyone in the industry.

Fortunately the film-makers in other countries saw Raindance as a way to launch into Europe and

How To Be A Successful Actor. Becoming an Actorpreneur.

into London. The Festival has grown to the point where we outgrew various venues and are now housed in the largest independent cinema in the West End - The Apollo.

In 1998 I started the British Independent Film Awards for a similar reason: to promote British films and film-makers. This event has grown to become a keynote in the UK's film industry calendar.

Of course, none of this wouldn't have been possible without a few generous benefactors and team of colleagues and collaborators unequalled in passion or ability in London.

Raindance is still proudly independent, and without any government support.

Is this the worst time for film-makers?

This is far from the worst time for film-makers. In fact, I think it is the very best time for film-makers. IPTV and online distribution have kicked the old boys' distribution model to pieces enabling anyone with good visual storytelling ability and simple and inexpensive camera gear to make a movie and get many *many* people to see it.

It seems that every film-maker comes into Raindance at some point. How does it feel to be the founder of such a creative hub?

I can't take any credit for the hundreds of successful film-makers I have been fortunate enough to meet at Raindance. Except to say that I, and my hard-working colleagues, are rewarded daily by meeting or speaking to the most talented people one could ever hope to meet. And that is reward enough for us!

How important is the internet and how can film-makers make the most of it?

There are two types of film-makers: Those who loathe and fear the internet and social media, and those who embrace it. Any film-maker or film festival without an online strategy is doomed in my opinion.

Advice for film-makers?

Elliot Grove: To make it as a film-maker, you need to:

➤ be a great story teller
➤ be able to get your hands on a bit of money
➤ develop excellent interpersonal and communication skills
➤ be firm and be strong enough to draw the line when someone makes unrealistic demands of you
➤ understand and develop a strong social media presence
➤ have boundless energy and be able to work 100 hour weeks
➤ talent helps too, but is the least essential of anything on this list

Who should we watch out for?

I am always asked who to watch out for. I really don't single out individual film-makers. we do, however, premiere about 75 features and 150 shorts each year by the most talented film-makers we have found during the past 12 months.

I returned from Brussels at the end of June and I met some extremely interesting 'Roger Corman' type producers there and this was most unusual and most welcome.

Several Belgian films will be playing at the Festival this year.

Jason Croot. Actor, film director and producer.

I have worked with Jason Croot quite a few times. Both as an actor on a film he was directing, and also as a director who cast him in my film. Prose & Cons. Jason is one of the most proactive actors I have ever met and he is already making his mark in a tough industry.

How did you get into making films?

I guess it started 10 years ago I made an experimental short film then made a few more and then progressed into professional features.

What is your background?

I started acting 10 years ago before that I had around 30 jobs. I never could settle in one but I guess I use a lot of life experience in my films and acting.

How did you get your first film off the ground?

Le Fear was a real whirlwind. Three weeks after coming up with the idea, the film was in the can, it was a great experience and really made my love for film-making grow much stronger; we were stuck in post-production for a while then the film was picked up for distribution. I'm awaiting the release date which will be great.

You act, write and direct, which one is your favourite?

I really can't pick between acting and directing. I would say acting is like my first love and will never end, film making was my bit on the side during the acting years but now has become my full time love affair.

You will be making *Le Fear, Le Sequel* soon. What was the idea behind the film?

I was walking to the supermarket one day and had this idea to make a film about a film, using my experiences as an actor I was on one film shoot and the sound guy was texting during a take, I put a lot of misfits together and it worked out well, *Le Sequel* is the follow up to the first film. This time

How To Be A Successful Actor. Becoming an Actorpreneur.
I've had longer to plan and develop the storyline.

What are you up to at the moment?

I'm in the middle of co directing my fourth feature film, *Meeting Place*. The film is based in a restaurant and follows conversations of 80 different actors some of whom play 2 characters. It's been a good shoot.

Who are your favourite actors/directors?

I have so many but to narrow down some, Steve McQueen, Max Von Sydow, Peter Sellers, early De Niro, Pacino and Brando, Jean-Pierre Léaud, Gérard Depardieu and the wonderful Roberto Benigni, directors Olivier Assayas, Jim Jarmusch, Ingmar Bergman, Martin Scorsese and Quentin Tarantino.

What advice to you have to people who want to get into film?

I guess, never give in no matter what and don't rely on anyone but yourself.

What is your favourite thing about the film industry?

Being on set as an actor or director and working it.

And the least?

Recalls. Just bloody cast me! (A recall is a second audition. Also called a callback. Means you are one step closer to the role. There can be more than one callback).

Thank you for taking the time to read this find out more on me on IMDB http://www.imdb.com/name/nm2907429/

Vanessa Bailey. Actor.
I interviewed Vanessa on what it is like juggling having children with a career.

Tell us about you

I'm a professional actress, specialising in screen acting. I have no formal acting training of any consequence. I read Education with Music and English at University and went into teaching straight after graduating. I'd also got married in my first year (at the tender age of nineteen) and am still happily married, now with three teenagers. I also have a dippy dog, grumpy rabbit and mercenary cat.

I'm forty-three and have been acting professionally with an agent for about three years. I came into acting through the back door, ignoring all the people who told me I wouldn't make it unless I went to Drama School. Finances and having a family made that option an impossibility. A combination of dogged determination, blind ignorance and luck meant that I did crack the system (starting off my career path as variously right elbow, left knee or back-of-head in the hallowed corridors of Casualty), gained Spotlight membership and secured an agent.

How hard is it to juggle acting with having children?

Without the amazing support of my husband I wouldn't be able to manage it. He works from home, mostly, so is able to cover any school runs that clash with auditions or work. But my children always come first. If one of them is ill, my priority is to care for them. If they need me to be at home then that's where I am. The main difference having a family is that I don't do the evening socialising and networking. We all need that time together and evenings are very busy. So unless it's essential for me to be somewhere, actor-related social activities are off-limits. Which means I miss out on lots of screenings, events etc... But that's just the way it is.

Do you think having children harmed your career?

I think it's helped. When you have restrictions on your time you have to be very clear about how you make decisions about which jobs you do. I think it's saved me from doing work that probably wouldn't have been particularly helpful in the grand scheme of things.

I also have a slice of life experience that is incredible. The intensity of maternal love is a unique, all-consuming dynamic. There's nothing like it. Knowing the fear of losing that source of love. Knowing you would kill or die for those children. All these things channel into your work. And having seen the incredible love and support my husband has shown me in supporting my dreams has been an eye-opener, too. He's put up with a lot from me!

What do you do if you have an audition?

Again, all the kids are at school and my husband will always get them there or pick them up if I can't (we drive them each morning and back in the evening), so that's usually not too problematic. Unless he's unavailable. In which case I don't attend the audition.

Are you open about the fact you have children?

Absolutely! If asked - though I don't chunter on about them, that's boring! I wouldn't take them to auditions either, unless I had absolutely no other option. It happened once in the school holidays, I took my youngest. He just sat and did his homework. I have been to auditions where women have taken their over-tired and on-the-loose toddlers with them and asked the other actors to mind them while they go in for their audition. That's very unfair on the actors who are trying to concentrate on their own audition.

Do you think men have the same pressure about juggling work and family?

The financial pressures must be enormous and I know male actors my age who struggle with not being able to earn and yet still having to justify attending castings. I think each family works differently within their own unique circumstances and they have to find what is the best arrangement for them as a family. Your family is the most precious thing.

If any actors are wondering if they should have children, what advice would you give them?

I would say something slightly controversial here: that if you are wondering whether you want to risk your career, then you're not really ready to have children. I don't mean the little flutters of nervousness we have making these decisions, but if it's a strong feeling that you still want to be able to fit children around your work, then wait. They don't fit around your work. They don't fit around anything! They get ill, get nits, have school concerts, need help with homework. Everything changes, and I wouldn't want to put myself under the pressure of being a new Mum and handling the kind of job this is. Mine were all at school full-time when I went into acting and that was a great blessing. For them! If my acting journey has taught me anything it's that you can have an acting career after you've had kids and over the age of forty!

Amanda from Actz Agency

Amanda is an excellent agent and wonderful person who runs the Actz Agency. She has got me some really good auditions. She gives some really amazing answers below. Even I learned something.

What is the best way for an actor to approach an agent?

Approaching an agent is most regularly done via email these days. Personally I like that method as it means we can deal with the request when it is most convenient to us. However, some actors still will ring and ask if it is okay for them to forward CVs and headshots via email or post before they actually send anything. That does get them extra Brownie Points because it means they are being very professional in their approach. We do notice those who still send hard copies through the post because they are in a minority. It is definitely a good way to stand out from the crowd. We always need CVs and headshots so just telephoning alone isn't a suitable option.

What is the best way for an actor to approach an agent?

In order for the actor to be noticeable to us they have to make themselves stand out in one way or another. We get several applications (5 to 10 generally) on a daily basis and the majority are totally unmemorable. A simple, 'Please see my attached CV and headshot' certainly doesn't attract us to them.

Firstly the headshot has to be professional and good. Seeing their eyes is a must. It must be just the head and preferably face forward. If it catches the actor's personality then even better. A poor headshot indicates an unprofessional approach to a career and so they are out before we've even looked at what skills and experience they have to offer.

Assuming we like the headshot and feel they have a look we'd like then we look at what they've written in support of their application. I guess different agents look for different things but we personally look for things that show they will fit in to the Actz Family. They need to show they are team players and are totally committed to their career. *Knowing they've researched about Actz rather than just sent a bulk email to loads of agents is also important.* We don't want someone who is desperate just to get any agent (though of course we understand that actors do have to contact many in order to get one) but rather an actor who feels Actz is what he or she is looking for. They definitely need to say that they feel they could be an asset to Act'z for one reason or another too.

I understand that not everyone is great with words and males especially don't go in to as much detail as females in general but there has to have been effort made to support their application.

So now we've seen a nice headshot and a reasonable supporting statement so we'll look further and see the CV. I don't need to tell you really what a good example of a CV is as there's none better than yours. Good skills make actors stand out because generally most will have similar work on their CVs and so it is the extras that make them different to the next actor. Personally I am happy to work with actors to make their CVs better, but I do like to see they've thought about their skillset as well as their work.

SPOTLIGHT!!!! If they aren't on there then most agents won't look twice. We have some who are not on there but won't look at any new ones who aren't. It shows professionalism and commitment. If they can't be bothered to join Spotlight in aid of their career then they are expecting something for nothing.

It is a hard business for those who do everything possible to help themselves so those not willing to do something like that aren't going to be any use to themselves or an agent I am afraid.

My next trick is to ask a few questions via email. I'm not so worried about the responses as I am about the length of time taken to get response. Because Act'z is very much about good communication between actor and ourselves we need to see that will be the case. If we have to wait ages for any additional info that we require then it doesn't bode well for that future relationship. Again we're aware that guys may not be quite as on the ball as ladies in that respect. That sounds sexist I am afraid but isn't meant detrimentally.

Describe an average day

An average day starts around 7.30am (I believe many agents begin later as a lot of the industry professionals really only come to life around 10am). We check emails initially. There will often be applications in with those first batch of emails so we'll have a look through those before filing them for rejection or further investigation.

We'll also be checking the emails to see if any auditions have come via that route.

Actors may also have emailed in with queries or updates. We'll deal with as many of those as

How To Be A Successful Actor. Becoming an Actorpreneur.

possible before starting to suggest people for roles.

Initially we'll deal with any directly emailed briefs. Spotlight then takes priority for our suggestions but after those are done we'll look at other casting sites and any other info we might have at our disposal. Emailing casting directors or phoning them will tend to begin after 10am.

What we do find though is that our early starts do catch the odd casting director at work before the rest of them are and before other agents are working. We've got a lot of work that way.

Throughout the main part of the day we will generally just be doing a combination of emailing clients, producers, directors, casting directors, telephoning and answering calls from the same and sometimes going out to meetings with any of the above. Andrew does headshots, showreels and website duties and Emma does as I do but concentrates primarily on stage work when both of us are here working. Generally my day will end between 6.30pm and 7pm as casting directors do still book actors in for castings until at least 6.30pm. We do still send hard copies of headshots and CVs off to casting directors/producers etc. but these tend to be more in respect of theatre than anything else.

Is there a lot of work out there?

The amount of work out there varies. Time of year affects it, e.g. August is always quiet. The reason for that is partly that everyone is up at the Fringe and partly because producers choose summer months for shooting to take advantage of the longer days. Any work for those shoots tends to be organised earlier in the year. Recession also affects things. We're finding that advertisers are choosing to use commercials again and pay additional usage to actors rather than having the cost of making a completely new commercial. That's great for those actors who are getting seen on screen for longer time periods and who are therefore also getting additional cash for not working again. It isn't so good for letting other actors get work, though. We do depend quite a lot on commercials to bring in regular good money. Stage is also a good way of us having a regular income coming in. Despite the odd dip in work generally we're managing to find a fair amount of it out there.

Is there still more work for men?

Yes, it is very frustrating that there is still far more work for men than women. Some companies are beginning to recognise that and are trying to redress the balance. Planet Rabbit are brilliant at writing many roles in for the ladies for example.

How often should an actor write to casting directors? What else can they do to help their career?

I would say a couple of times a year, or perhaps around 9 monthly is sufficient to write to a casting director. Postcards are a terrific idea. We find that a postcard sized headshot with the actor's details and agent's details on the back is a brilliant way of attracting good attention. It doesn't need a CV but your Spotlight pin is good to have on it.

Other things to improve the actors' chances have probably already been mentioned above. Spotlight, good CV, good headshot and an agent for a start.

How To Be A Successful Actor. Becoming an Actorpreneur.

Keeping doing training helps keep the actor fresh and also adds to skills. Don't spend a fortune on it but find things that interest you and will give you skills that you're missing.

Getting together in groups with other actors can also help. Perhaps doing bits of filming together or putting on shows. Anything really that keeps the actor busy and mixing with other actors and professionals is good, even if not paid. Having said that I only mean if it is work generated by yourself. I am not advocating doing a lot of unpaid work for unscrupulous producers who want something for nothing.

Can the actor learn a new skill entirely? A sport? A musical or dance skill? The more skills there are on the CV the better. There really are loads of actors out there all with very similar CVs, so the actor needs to stand out by having great skills.

Something unusual or funny on the CV is a good way to stand out too. Camel riding, archery or something even weirder like juggling glass bottles of milk with one hand, Jack Russell dogs with the other, whilst standing on your head would certainly get a laugh and get the actor noticed!!! Yes, I know that's ridiculous but you know what I am trying to get at.

Of course these things all aid the actor to get a chance to get seen by people who matter. Once given that chance there's a whole lot of things the actor needs to do to ensure they at least don't blow their chances as soon as they walk in the door. Punctuality, politeness and being dressed appropriately would appear to be common sense things but you'd be surprised how many actors fall short even at that stage. The number who fail to turn up at all is staggering in view of how difficult it is to get that opportunity in the first place. Casting directors don't need to give actors a second chance as they have so many actors to choose from.

What advice can you give to an actor who has just left drama school?

Leaving drama school is exciting and yet daunting. We are amazed how many come out thinking they will be famous immediately just because they've been to drama school. It can be a very hard lesson to learn that this business is all about hard work and determination, as well as some talent and a lot of luck thrown in there for good measure. My main advice would be to be prepared to work extremely hard. Find a good agent who offers what you need. Don't ever pay for representation or for castings.

What advice can you give to an actor?

I think the one area where actors generally fall short is with staying power. It is difficult and when you've been sat there months without an audition or have gone to loads of auditions and haven't got work, it can be extremely difficult to stay positive and remain focused. Those who find that within themselves are the ones who ultimately make it.

Not over-analysing rejection is important too. There's nothing wrong with looking at what you did and seeing ways it could be improved but be careful not to think you must be rubbish because you didn't get a role. There are so many reasons people don't get roles, and mostly nothing to do with their ability as an actor.

What is the best thing an actor can do for their career?

How To Be A Successful Actor. Becoming an Actorpreneur.

Being proactive, determined and focused are the best things an actor can do for their career. Probably I should say having a good agent :)

And the worst?

Letting any professional in the industry down, i.e. not turning up for a casting or for work, is the worst thing an actor can do for their career.

Mason Kayne

Mason Kayne is a brilliant actor. He played the young Gene Hunt in Ashes to Ashes and I also cast him in my film Prose & Cons. This is what Mason has to say about the industry.

What made you go into acting?

To be honest, I don't actually remember making a conscious decision to go into acting. It was more like acting chose me. I had been doing it for many years as a hobby, appearing in the school shows and the local amateur dramatics. For some reason acting just seemed to suit my personality.

What's your favourite job so far?

Ashes to Ashes of course! We had an amazing crew, an amazing cast, amazing writing and it was just so much fun to be on!

And your least?

Hmm, I think I would have to say a short film I agreed to do when I first came out of drama school. I was keen to get clips for my showreel and just said yes to the first thing that came along. The script was terrible and the director and crew were inexperienced. There was very little hope in making it a good film. It was a rookie error to agree to it, but I'm glad that I made the mistake so that I know NOT to repeat it in the future.

Favourite actors?

I couldn't possibly say! There are too many to list! I admire any actor that I feel safe with, anyone that I can watch and not have any doubts in my mind that I am about to be entertained.

Tell me about *Ashes to Ashes*

127

Ashes was probably the most fun I've ever had on a project to date. There was just this fantastic vibe to the atmosphere, like everything there just fit together perfectly. We had a fantastic cast, the crew were very professional, everyone was friendly and the storyline looked amazing. It felt like a true honour to be a part of the production.

What do you think of the industry at the moment?

If I'm honest I'm not entirely sure what to think of the industry at the moment. It seems to be lacking in a logical structure.

Gone are the days where you could start out in rep theatre and work your way up the ladder so I can understand how many young aspiring performers find it difficult to work out where to begin in an acting career.

These days as young actors, people seem to be very keen to pigeonhole us quite early on in our careers, or 'type' us so to speak, so that we end up playing similar roles. And politics in the acting game seem to be quite illogical at times too. It's almost like people are terrified to take a chance of any kind these days, so they stick with safe decisions. Talent scouts no longer seem to exist either. It all seems to boil down to what drama school you went to and how successful your last show was.

Did you train? Do you recommend it?

I did indeed train but I never finished the course. One thing that was bugging me about drama school was that they focused primarily on the performing skills and neglected to teach us how to function in the industry. It also bothered me how I felt like I was living in a bubble and that my fate was, to a certain extent, out of my control. Don't get me wrong, I'm not dead set against drama training, It sure as hell doesn't do you any harm, it just wasn't for me. I learn better from hands-on experience, so I cannot recommend it, but I don't discourage it either.

What is your advice for aspiring actors?

I'm of the mind that if you want to be an actor, then don't do it. If you're going to be an actor, then do it. It sounds petty, but that slight difference in attitude makes all the difference. Loads of people want to be actors, but only a small percentage will actually go out and do it, so get out there, dive in, explore options, make mistakes, learn from them, and for the love of God don't let anyone tell you: 'You'll never succeed as an actor'.

What's next?

Well, now that I'm all fired up from answering that last question, I'm going to follow my own advice from above, dive back in and I'll see you in theatre or on screen at some point.

Richard Evans Casting director.

Richard Evans is a brilliant casting director whose book Auditions: A Practical Guide *is essential reading.*

How did you get into casting?

I worked as assistant to two casting directors, but I'd always had a casting director's brain (I used to read Spotlight in the local library from the age of 8, which, although it sounds sad, completely fascinated me!). I started on my own in 1989, as the first freelance casting director to specialise in theatre - in those days, the vast majority of theatre casting was done by artistic directors and their secretaries, and was not considered worthy of specialised casting knowledge (the only people who cast for theatre worked in the casting departments of the major companies, such as the RSC and The National Theatre, and the only other freelancer was Leonie Cosman who did many of the West End musicals). While many film and TV casters initially treated theatre with disdain, viewpoints changed remarkably quickly, so I, in turn, diversified, but theatre is still my favourite medium.

Favourite film you have cast?

I've cast relatively few films, as it's not really a medium that I've pushed to work in. I am, however, extremely proud of most of the projects I've cast, for a multitude of reasons.

What do you love about your job?

Getting it right! Leaving a casting where we have first, second, third... even eighth choices for each character makes me walk on air. I always strive for absolute perfection and sweat blood over everything I do, so when everything falls into place it makes it all worthwhile. My absolute favourite thing is giving someone their first job out of drama school and then seeing them progress to bigger and better things - it doesn't often happen, as there aren't always suitable roles on my desk at the right time, but it's amazing when it does.

Advice for actors?

Buy my book!... no, seriously... BUY MY BOOK! Where do I start?! Be honest about your capabilities and what you've done. We are in a small business, which gets smaller the longer you are in it, so any fibs will surely be found out. Prepare everything thoroughly, know as much as you can about the projects you're up for and the industry you're in. Be prepared for anything, and, above all, enjoy whatever you do - if you don't, others won't. I could go on, but there's lots of other advice, tips and resources at www.auditionsapracticalguide.com

Who is your inspiration?

Anyone who knows what they want and goes for it wholeheartedly... especially if they have overcome adversity to do so.

What's next?

How To Be A Successful Actor. Becoming an Actorpreneur.

I'm currently in discussions to cast a new musical, which it's hoped will tour the UK in early 2011, and I'm told that a corporate video has had its budget approved, six months after I was first called about it. My policy is to always believe that a project is only definite after it has happened and the cheque has cleared. People are being far more cautious at the moment, due to the recession, but the great thing about our Industry is you never know when the phone will ring and your luck will change - even after all these years, I am frequently surprised when it happens to me.

Tell me about your book.
AUDITIONS: A PRACTICAL GUIDE is, I'm told, just that. I wanted to write a book that is an easy and amusing read and would be useful and pertinent to every performer, from those considering training or starting a career in performing arts to the most experienced actors who want to brush up their skills and learn new techniques. The reaction has been phenomenally positive, even from people who have been in the industry for decades and are notoriously harsh critics (I'm still waiting for someone to contact me and say 'I didn't like your book because...', which would actually be quite refreshing, silly though that may sound). The book covers many different genres and takes the reader through the audition process step by step. Writing this book was a long-held ambition - I first thought of writing it back in 1993 - and was a huge learning curve, taking over 4 years from conception to publication. I wanted to write it partly as I was frustrated at the amount of performers who unwittingly lose jobs by auditioning badly and, on a more selfish note, because I wanted to prove to myself that I could write a book and get it published. It is without doubt the proudest achievement of my life... so far!

What is your background?

I was an actor for 10 years, which I believe has stood me in excellent stead to work in casting, as, having seen things from both sides of the audition table, I am able to appreciate everyone's point of view and, hopefully get the best out of performers when auditioning.

What does your average day consist of?

There's really no such thing as an average day, every day is different and that's the way I like it. I'm usually at my desk by around 10am, replying to emails that have come in overnight and ploughing through my daily to do list. Some days are frantic, others very quiet, there's no pattern. I go to the theatre to keep abreast of actors' work at least 3 or 4 nights a week and may then return to my desk afterwards to catch up, especially if I'm dealing with agents and producers in America.

Favourite actors?

My favourite actors are mainly those that I like as people as well as for their skill as performers. There are many, and most aren't the least bit famous or even yet in the public eye, so I'll spare their blushes by mentioning them and having you saying 'Who?'. Those you may have heard of include: Douglas Hodge who is terrific and starting to be given the recognition he deserves, having been awarded best actor on both sides of the Atlantic for his astounding performance as Albin in *La Cage Aux Folles*. Samantha Morton always gives wonderfully naturalistic performances; Daniel Radcliffe is really proving himself to be a great actor (he's also not a bad magician in real life!); Sheridan Smith has been excellent in everything I've see her do; Julie Walters is far more versatile than most people ever see, and Alec McCowen is doubtless the most underrated actor of his generation, if not all time.

What is the hardest part of the job?

Getting performers to prepare adequately for auditions and recalls, especially when they've been sent sides or songs to learn... and also getting some companies to pay my invoices on time!

Alison Winter. Actor and writer.

Alison is a very talented actor and writer. I cast her in a music video in 2008. She has experience in LA and London.

Tell us a bit about you

I am a writer and actress, originally from Reading.

What made you move to LA?

It kept being suggested as a better option by people I was working with over a few years, and then was followed up by an odd chain of events and coincidences until I finally took the first step.

How easy was the process?

For me it was quite easy. There are some organisations in place to help you make the move. They set up a sort of introduction to LA and prepare you for a showcase audition with various agencies. I wasn't prepared to move there unless I knew I had representation, though I did meet some actors who had found an agent at a later stage.

How hard/easy was it to get a visa?

It's not an easy thing but isn't difficult as much as lengthy and involved. It will always take time and effort, just weathering that bureaucratic process. There are lots of places that recommend good lawyers who will keep you informed. Patience is the key.

What was the biggest surprise when you moved to LA?

Just how blue the sky was. And then perhaps how expensive cars are.

What was living in LA like?

It's like nothing else. It's an alien world - even to my American friends who had come from all over the States. At first it takes a while to adjust to the scale of it. For our British minds it's worth saying that LA is more like a county than what we would understand as a city; many towns connected by a network of motorways. You spend a lot of time in your car, though the traffic is never worse than here. It's just that places are so far apart.

What is the reaction to British actors in LA?

How To Be A Successful Actor. Becoming an Actorpreneur.

It's a cliché but it's the truth. Everyone loves a Brit. I call it favourable racism. As actors we have a reputation for being well trained and hardworking (probably because of the theatre thing) and then people just love the accent. So we're very welcome, though anyone will tell you that however much they love your Britishness, it wears off quickly if you can't master an American standard accent, and that is much harder than most people realise.

Top tips for actors moving to LA?

Be prepared to spend a lot of money. Moving to LA, you won't have a California credit rating (Americans from other States have this issue too). This will mean paying deposits up front for everything; accommodation, bills, etc. It will mean financing a car is complicated if you can't buy it outright. And you do need a car as an actor, or you will struggle to get to last minute auditions sometimes 20 miles apart or find that you actually cannot get somewhere because the only way is via the freeway.

It is a very transient city, so stick to your guns. Most people and things around you will come and go, but you will find out who and what can or will stay.

How easy is it to find work?

There are many actor websites that post about various jobs. It's just more of the same. The big jobs are as elusive as ever. But there are always people looking to create work. The more people you meet, the more opportunity there is.

Would you recommend other actors move to LA?

It depends on the person. I've met actors out there who have been very successful in the UK or elsewhere, but LA just doesn't care. The flipside is that people who can't get a break in the UK may find they're a precious commodity over there. It is a lottery in both places. LA is just a bigger game. So you have to work out if you think it would be worth the move for you. If it continuously bugs you then maybe it's worth giving it a go just for peace of mind and knowing you tried. That's not bad for a bottom line.

You are back in London now. Is the acting industry easier here?

I don't think it's any easier here - it's a lot smaller and more closed than LA. However, London suits me personally. I'm also a writer so I like cosy evenings where I get to write. I love the city and being able to walk around, take in concerts and theatre which I really missed. I go back to LA maybe twice a year and continue developing projects mostly as a writer now.

What's next for you?

At the moment I am spending most of my time writing then networking. I am doing a lot with Women in Film and TV here in London. I found Women in Film (LA) to be the most helpful organisation in LA as everyone is very work focused (rather than schmoozing), so I followed that up here too. As with LA, I have found that the best way to find work is to

132

How To Be A Successful Actor. Becoming an Actorpreneur.

create it, so that is what I am up to for the next 6 months.

Lance Carter.

*Lance is an actor and also the editor of Daily Actor (http:/*dailyactor.com*), an amazing website about acting. It has lots of interviews and tips so check it out. Lance acts in Los Angeles and here he gives us a perspective from across the pond.*

Tell us a bit about you and also DailyActor.com (which is one of my fav sites!)

Well, I'm originally from Maryland and that's where I got my start. I started with theatre, got my SAG card, booked some TV and films and eventually moved to LA.

I started the website a couple years ago. It was originally going to be just a blog about my auditions and acting life but I quickly got bored with that. I read a ton of sites and I'm an entertainment news junkie...so, one day I just posted some news on the site. I noticed I got a couple comments on the posts and started posting things regularly..... and now here we are.

You have a portfolio career, would you ever want to be just an actor?

Yeah, totally. I mean, that's my priority but acting - at least for me - has a lot of downtime. I go to classes and workshops but I still have a lot of free time. So, this is the next best option.

How do your different careers add to one another.

It's actually part of the reason I got my current agent. I've interviewed a ton of actors, directors, producers and casting directors and listed them when I sent my cover letter. I've had some auditions from the people I've interviewed... so, yeah. Some good things have come out of it.

What have you learned about acting?

I don't know if I've learned anything about acting in general. What I've learned has all been about the acting 'business.' Most specifically, create your own work. Don't let the work come to you.

What is the best thing an actor can do for their career?

Like I said above, create your own work. Create a web series, shoot a short film, write something. Be creative and keep your juices flowing.

And the worst?

How To Be A Successful Actor. Becoming an Actorpreneur.

Waiting for the phone to ring.

What advice do you have for aspiring actor.

Again, create your own work. Do theatre. And, get out there and make friends with your peers.

What was your favourite acting job?

They've all been pretty darn good.

Acting tips?

Always have a beginning, middle and end to your scene. Even if it's one line.

Audition tips?

Be nice to EVERYONE in the room. Try and come in as memorized as you can. Have fun because they want you to do well!

What is the best way to stay sane in the acting industry?

Don't make it your whole entire life. Have other hobbies and interests! ... and develop a love of tequila.

Chapter 19: Quotes

Here are some of my favourite quotes on acting that I have come across.

I think in our business, you're likely to feel that way. Letting go of your vanity is not easy. But if that character wore makeup, you'd never believe her. Anyway, with actors, all our ages are out there for all to see—you can't hide anything, really. And it's kind of a relief. This is my age, this is what I look like without makeup on—who cares? That youth culture—that lying about your age—it's all denial of death anyway.
- Julianne Moore on roughing it for a part. (Source: http://www.lancecarter.net/daily/2012/08/24/julianne-moore-carrie-actors-aging/)

Without wonder and insight, acting is just a business. With it, it becomes creation.
- Bette Davis (Source: http://www.bettedavis.com/about/quotes.html)

Acting is standing up naked and turning around very slowly.
- Rosalind Russell (http://www.brainyquote.com/quotes/quotes/r/rosalindru137406.html)

Acting is not about being someone different. It's finding the similarity in what is apparently different, then finding myself in there.
-Meryl Streep (Source: http://www.newspapers.com/newspage/1707773/)

An ounce of behaviour is worth a pound of words.
- Sanford Meisner (Source: http://www.ruskinschool.com/ruskin-favorites/quotes)

My job is usually to express emotion as freely as possible.
- Meryl Streep (Source: http://www.ace-your-audition.com/acting-quotes.html)

I'm curious about other people. That's the essence of my acting. I'm interested in what it would be like to be you.
- Meryl Streep (Source: http://www.brainyquote.com/quotes/authors/m/meryl_streep_2.html)

I think the most liberating thing I did early on was to free myself from any concern with my looks as they pertain to my work.
- Meryl Streep (Source: http://www.brainyquote.com/quotes/quotes/m/merylstree369295.html)

Show me a great actor and I'll show you a lousy husband. Show me a great actress, and you've seen the devil.
- W. C. Fields (Source: http://www.brainyquote.com/quotes/quotes/w/wcfields151499.html)

I love acting. It is so much more real than life.
- Oscar Wilde (Source: http://www.goodreads.com/quotes/21324-i-love-acting-it-is-so-much-more-real-than)

How To Be A Successful Actor. Becoming an Actorpreneur.

I'm a skilled professional actor. Whether or not I've any talent is beside the point. - Michael Caine
(Source: http://www.brainyquote.com/quotes/authors/m/michael_caine.html)

The word theatre comes from the Greeks. It means the seeing place. It is the place people come to see the truth about life and the social situation.
- Stella Adler (Source: http://en.wikipedia.org/wiki/Stella_Adler)

There's nothing more boring than unintelligent actors, because all they have to talk about is themselves and acting. There have to be other things.
- Tim Robbins (Source: http://quotes.lifehack.org/quote/tim-robbins/theres-nothing-more-boring-than-unintelligent-actors/)

Life beats down and crushes the soul and art reminds you that you have one.
- Stella Adler (Source: http://en.wikipedia.org/wiki/Stella_Adler)

So, we are now at the end. I hope you enjoyed the book and it helps you in your career. Please contact me at www.catherinebalavage.com if you have any comments or want to know more about me. Break a leg!

About The Author

Catherine Balavage is an actress in her late twenties. She has worked as an actor for over ten years. She has worked in film, television, theatre and voiceover. She performed three different roles in one play on the West End, beat up Paul McGann in Luther and has worked with Scorsese and Eddie Marsan.

She also writes, produces and directs, with her first full length feature, Prose & Cons, coming out this year. She writes about the truth of the acting industry, from an insiders point of view, and as someone who didn't do the proper training, grew up in a small Scottish town, and had no contacts in the industry before she started. It is an indispensable guide to the business of acting.

Thanks to my family first and foremost: my parents, brothers and my husband James. Thank you to my nephew just for being cute and adorable. You have all been so supportive and I love you so much. Thank you to Clea Myers, everyone who let me interview them or gave advice, Amy Hubbard, Jessica Manins from Starnow, Emma Dyson from Spotlight and Simon from Casting Call Pro. Steve McAleavy who did the cover, Margaret and Dick Graham for their massive contribution, Penny Deacon for editing and the wonderful review. Lastly, but not least, every single one of my friends who either bought the book. You are all amazing and I could not have done it without you. I also want to thank anyone I have forgotten: it doesn't mean I don't love and appreciate you.

Printed in Great Britain
by Amazon.co.uk, Ltd.,
Marston Gate.